New Directions for
Community Colleges

Arthur M. Cohen
EDITOR-IN-CHIEF

Florence B. Brawer
ASSOCIATE EDITOR

Pam Schuetz
PUBLICATIONS COORDINATOR

Legal Issues in the Community College

Robert C. Cloud
EDITOR

Number 125 • Spring 2004
Jossey-Bass
San Francisco

LEGAL ISSUES IN THE COMMUNITY COLLEGE
Robert C. Cloud (ed.)
New Directions for Community Colleges, no. 125

Arthur M. Cohen, Editor-in-Chief
Florence B. Brawer, Associate Editor

NEW DIRECTIONS FOR COMMUNITY COLLEGES (ISSN 0194-3081, electronic ISSN 1536-0733) is part of The Jossey-Bass Higher and Adult Education Series and is published quarterly by Wiley Subscription Services, Inc., A Wiley Company, at Jossey-Bass, 989 Market Street, San Francisco, California 94103-1741. Periodicals Postage Paid at San Francisco, California, and at additional mailing offices. POSTMASTER: Send address changes to New Directions for Community Colleges, Jossey-Bass, 989 Market Street, San Francisco, California 94103-1741.

SUBSCRIPTIONS cost $80.00 for individuals and $165.00 for institutions, agencies, and libraries. Prices subject to change. See order form in back of book.

EDITORIAL CORRESPONDENCE should be sent to the Editor-in-Chief, Arthur M. Cohen, at the Graduate School of Education and Information Studies, University of California, Box 951521, Los Angeles, California 90095-1521. All manuscripts receive anonymous reviews by external referees.

New Directions for Community Colleges is indexed in Current Index to Journals in Education (ERIC).

Microfilm copies of issues and articles are available in 16mm and 35mm, as well as microfiche in 105mm, through University Microfilms Inc., 300 North Zeeb Road, Ann Arbor, Michigan 48106-1346.

CONTENTS

EDITOR'S NOTES

Community colleges are being sued with increasing frequency over a wide range of issues. Many of those issues, including governing board relations, academic freedom, and employment matters, are not new to postsecondary education institutions. Other legal issues are newer to community college campuses, yet they are equally perplexing and confounding. Student rights, codes of conduct, accommodation of disabled students, safety on the campus, intellectual property rights, distance education, and risk management are examples of these newer and evolving areas of legal contention. Trustees, administrators, and faculty must find ways to resolve these and other issues if community colleges are to continue providing exemplary services to students.

Without doubt, trustees and administrators function in a legalistic environment. Special-interest groups, including teachers' unions and taxpayers' associations, are increasingly involved in governing board elections, creating politically volatile situations for presidents and other administrators. Therefore, many presidents must deal with hostile faculties on one hand and divided trustees on the other. In addition, college leaders are confronted with a multitude of federal statutes and court rulings that—although necessary to ensure equal protection for all students—have made governance and administration more complex and legalistic than ever before.

Trustees and administrators are defendants in lawsuits of all types, including the frivolous and the ridiculous. Consequently, caution is a watchword among many presidents and their legal counsels. Some college attorneys advise administrators to assume that all personnel matters will lead to litigation and to act and keep records accordingly. Routine personnel actions now require meticulous documentation and consultation with counsel. Relatively innocuous matters formerly resolved through private consultation may now be litigated in federal district court. Colleges often prevail in court but at an enormous cost in resources, staff time, and campus morale. Presidents in some colleges may spend as much time on potentially volatile legal issues as they do on more traditional administrative functions like program development and fundraising.

The legalistic climate in many community college districts does nothing to foster the teamwork that is essential in quality institutions. College leaders must inform themselves and their colleagues about the legal issues that threaten institutional stability and effectiveness. This volume provides useful information on the scope and complexity of those issues. The intended

---

This volume offers an overview of some legal issues facing community colleges. For comprehensive guidance in specific situations, consult your legal counsel.

audience includes community college trustees, administrators, faculty, and other professional staff, such as human resource personnel and risk managers. Content will be of particular interest to college attorneys, government officials, and policymakers who may be concerned about the impact of the litigious climate on college resources and services to the public. Finally, the volume will be of interest to university faculty and graduate students in higher education programs.

Chapter One, by Ralph D. Mawdsley, describes the contractual nature of the relationship between students and their institutions. The Civil Rights Act of 1964, the Family Educational Rights and Privacy Act (FERPA), and student codes of conduct are discussed in terms of their relationship to institutional mission, student rights, and campus safety. The implications of academic and nonacademic misconduct are discussed, and the chapter concludes with a review of the minimum due process rights of students facing suspension or expulsion.

In Chapter Two, Constance S. Hawke describes the federal legal requirements for accommodating disabled students. *Disability, discrimination,* and other terms from Section 504 of the Rehabilitation Act of 1973 and the Americans with Disabilities Act of 1990 are defined. Hawke addresses equal access, admissions procedures, documentation, and types of accommodation. The chapter clarifies that the intent of federal law is to ensure equal educational opportunity for all disabled students—no more, no less. It concludes with examples of good practice.

In Chapter Three, Todd A. DeMitchell reviews federal laws shaping employment issues such as employee supervision, performance evaluation, contracts, and documentation. Affirmative action, age and gender discrimination, and sexual harassment are discussed. The chapter concludes with specific recommendations on effective employment policies and procedures and human resource management practices.

In Chapter Four, Richard J. Boris reviews the three-decade history of collective bargaining in the community colleges. Boris examines the impact of collective bargaining on college administrators, trustees, academic freedom, and faculty participation in governance. The chapter also addresses the relationship of faculty unions to the American labor movement and competition among the unions for faculty affiliations. Finally, the chapter offers suggestions for future collective bargaining efforts.

In Chapter Five, Richard Fossey and R. Craig Wood review the history and current status of academic freedom and tenure in postsecondary education, including the institution's autonomy to govern its affairs and the individual teacher's right to research, write, and speak freely. Fossey and Wood review recent court decisions that clarify a scholar's right to academic freedom in the context of publishing, researching, and engaging in classroom speech. The chapter includes a brief discussion of multiyear contracts and posttenure reviews as alternatives to the traditional tenure system.

In Chapter Six, Kenneth D. Salomon and Michael B. Goldstein discuss copyright issues in technology-mediated instruction. The chapter examines the distinction between individual property rights in traditional face-to-face instruction and those rights in the emerging context of electronic delivery systems. Changing federal law and policy are reviewed. The chapter concludes with an examination of emerging trends in intellectual property policies.

Chapter Seven, by Timothy K. Garfield, presents an overview of community college governing board legal issues. Garfield examines the authority of the board, rights of individual board members, internal and external communication, the importance of orientation and professional development activities for board members, and codes of ethics. The chapter closes with examples of exemplary and dysfunctional trustee behavior and offers specific suggestions for improving board effectiveness.

Chapter Eight, by Brett A. Sokolow, identifies and reviews major risk management strategies. Risk management is defined and discussed in terms of its importance in community college administration. Proper risk management policies and procedures are recommended.

Chapter Nine, by Carol Kozeracki, presents key resources on legal issues in the community colleges. An annotated bibliography of selected legal cases and a listing of legal resources are included for readers who wish to learn more about the subject. Faculty teaching graduate courses on the community college can use all or part of the resources as a reading list for students. Finally, this chapter also provides useful background material for administrators whose responsibilities may bring them into contact with legal issues.

In summary, this volume informs readers about the scope and complexity of the legal issues affecting American community colleges. In doing so, it fulfills a dual purpose. First, it provides a reliable reference source for administrators, trustees, and policymakers who need accurate information on current legal issues that threaten institutional resources and stability. Second, it offers scholars and aspiring administrators valuable information about the realities of community college leadership in the politicized and legalistic environment of the twenty-first century.

Robert C. Cloud
Editor

ROBERT C. CLOUD is professor of higher education at Baylor University. He is a former president of Lee College in Baytown, Texas.

1

Community college students, like students in all of higher education, find their relationship with the college defined by contract. However, this contract is shaped and influenced by rights granted under state and federal constitutions and statutes. Knowing what these rights are can assist college officials in avoiding unnecessary litigation.

Student Rights, Safety, and Codes of Conduct

Ralph D. Mawdsley

Courts of law have consistently found that the relationship between students and their postsecondary institutions is a contractual one (*Ross v. Creighton University*, 1992). Most commonly, a contract is a legal relationship between parties that is based on mutually enforceable written or oral promises. The purpose of this chapter is to discuss constitutional, statutory, contractual, and common law legal issues that affect a student's relationship with the community college.

Student Rights

Students have contractual rights under college rules, state law, and federal statute. Student handbooks and bulletins form the basis for most contractual litigation between students and colleges. In addition, the college-student contract can include statements found in the application, brochures, syllabi, other publications, and even oral statements made by faculty and administrators. As long as the statements are specific enough to enforce, courts will treat them as promises and enforce them. Where untruthful statements are made and students rely on them to their detriment, the students can also have claims for misrepresentation, fraud, and deceptive practices under state deceptive practices statutes.

Rights of Students as Consumers. The contractual relationship between students and their colleges forms the basis for treating students not only as participants in a contract but also as consumers of educational services. Recognition by courts that students may have claims as consumers is

New Directions for Community Colleges, no. 125, Spring 2004 © Wiley Periodicals, Inc.

a dramatic shift from viewing a college as bound by contract to individual students. A consumer rights approach views colleges as vendors (much like the manufacturers of football helmets) that can be regulated and be held responsible for the integrity of their educational product. Treatment of colleges as business vendors is best reflected in litigation where colleges are sued under state consumer protection legislation, such as deceptive practices statutes.

Courts expect that colleges will teach courses as advertised. Thus in *Dezick v. Umpqua Community College* (1979), a college's failure to offer an advanced welding program as advertised in a catalogue and as promised orally by the college's dean constituted fraudulent misrepresentation, resulting in damages awarded to a student. Because the student continued to enroll for three terms without ever being able to take the courses promised, the measure of damages was the amount of wages the student lost as a result of continuing in the college rather than having worked during those three terms.

Although faculty members have considerable latitude in determining the content of their courses, the content must fit within the course description set forth in college publications. A New York case, *Andre v. Pace University* (1994), addressed the tension between a faculty member's academic freedom and students' expectations of course content based on the university's catalogue. Where a tenured faculty member decided to teach a beginning-level computer programming course at a more advanced level than described in the catalogue, students who enrolled in the course were entitled to complete tuition refunds under negligent misrepresentation and breach of contract theories. Given the tendency at most community colleges to use large numbers of adjunct faculty, colleges should exercise careful supervision over course content in relation to published descriptions.

In *Cencor, Inc., v. Tolman* (1994), students had a breach of contract claim when a vocational school failed to provide specific educational services promised in the catalogue. Among the services promised were training on up-to-date equipment and instruments, supervision by qualified faculty, and inclusion of computer word processing as part of the curriculum. The normal measure of damages that colleges must pay to students who are successful in misrepresentation cases will be a refund of all tuition paid. However, punitive damages may be available if officials knew of the misrepresentation and had knowledge of a high degree of probability that students would be injured (*Troknya v. Cleveland Chiropractic Clinic*, 2002). Damages may also be available under consumer protection legislation, such as in *Andre*, where each student was entitled to $1,000 in punitive damages because the misrepresentation violated the state's deceptive practices statute.

Most states have deceptive practices statutes that are directed at punishing fraud against consumers. These statutes vary by state and should be examined carefully by community college officials. The New York statute, relied on in *Andre*, is troublesome in that it permits recovery even though students may not prove that a college's practices were intentional, fraudulent, or reckless, or that the students actually relied on the college's misrepresentations or deceptive practices. *Andre* is the best example of students' being treated as consumers by a court and of a college, having placed services in the marketplace, being deemed liable for the quality of those services. However, even though consumer protection statutes tend to be interpreted broadly by courts, the amount of recovery may be limited within the statute.

Due Process Rights. The Fourteenth Amendment to the U.S. Constitution provides that every person has property and liberty rights that cannot be restricted or denied without due process of law. Students do not shed their constitutional rights simply because they enter the campuses of community colleges to take courses. Instead, students enjoy constitutional rights that protect their property, liberty, procedural, and substantive rights while limiting the authority of college officials to make and enforce rules and regulations on campus.

Constitutional Property and Liberty Rights. Student property rights are entitlements or expectations grounded in the contractual relationship created as soon as a student is admitted to a college (*Mangla v. Brown University,* 1991). This property right forms the basis for an expectation that the student will not be removed from the college in an arbitrary or unfair manner. Liberty rights ensure that students' good name, reputation, integrity, and honor cannot be impugned without providing students with a hearing to clear their names. Charges involving misconduct generally raise concerns about these liberty rights, but providing a student with a hearing to address the truth or falsity of the charges serves to address the student's liberty right claim.

Constitutional Procedural Due Process Rights. Procedural due process rights relate to the treatment that students receive during the time frame surrounding and following an alleged failure to comply with college rules of conduct. Rights traditionally considered as procedural include notice of charges, notice of the time and place of the hearing, opportunities to present evidence, calling and cross-examining witnesses, the presence of an attorney or advocate, the right to an unbiased hearing tribunal, and a right to appeal an adverse ruling. However, students may not necessarily be entitled under the Constitution to all of these procedural rights.

The procedural rights to which a student is entitled are influenced by two key factors. First, college hearings that address student misconduct are considered by courts to be administrative rather than criminal. Therefore, students are not entitled to the same procedural due process that they could expect in a criminal proceeding (*Fellheimer v. Middlebury College,* 1994). Second, the amount of procedural due process is influenced by whether a rule violation is considered to be academic or disciplinary. Academic controversies deal with grade disputes, cheating, and plagiarism. Where students challenge grades given in a course, courts normally require only a minimal level of procedural due process (*Trahms v. Trustees of Columbia University*, 1997; *Williams v. State University of New York*, 1998). Because grade disputes tend to involve subjective faculty judgment, courts give considerable deference to colleges and their instructors (*Board of Curators of University of Missouri v. Horowitz*, 1978; *Regents of University of Michigan v. Ewing*, 1985; *Susan M. v. New York Law School*, 1990).

However, punishments for academic violations like cheating and plagiarism can be severe and include suspensions, expulsions, and degree revocations (*Flannery v. Board of Trustees of Illinois Community College*, 1996; *Dinu v. President and Fellows of Harvard College*, 1999). In these cases, the severity of the penalty influences the nature of the due process to which a student is entitled. Courts have held that due process in cheating and plagiarism cases requires an impartial judicial tribunal, the right to have an adviser present, the right to be present at the hearing and to cross-examine witnesses, and the right to an appeal to a high-level administrative official (*Clayton v. Princeton University*, 1985). However, students do not have a due process right to an attorney in an academic controversy hearing, and even if a student's attorney is permitted to attend a hearing, the attorney can be prohibited from cross-examining witnesses (*Hall v. Medical College of Ohio at Toledo*, 1984; *Crook v. Baker*, 1987).

Courts consider all other rule violations to be disciplinary and will require more due process protections than are required for academic controversies to ensure fairness (Mawdsley, 1994). Examples of disciplinary infractions include vandalism, assaults, and thefts on campus. Although the exact protections required by constitutional due process vary somewhat among courts, they frequently include cross-examination and right to an attorney (*Woodis v. Westark Community College*, 1998). In disciplinary disputes, students are entitled to the same degree of rights exercised by the college. Thus if the college has an attorney at a disciplinary hearing, the student can also have one present, and if the college's attorney can cross-examine, so can the student's (*Crook v. Baker*, 1987).

Though courts suggest less due process for academic misconduct, penalties such as expulsion and degree revocations are at least as severe as what a student could receive for a disciplinary violation. As a result, community college officials might be well advised to provide the same degree of due process protection for academic controversies as for disciplinary violations on the theory that some courts may be responsive to a student claim that equality of punishment should require equality of due process.

Although community colleges cannot offer less than the constitutional minimum in their student handbooks, they may accord students due process rights that go beyond the constitutional minimum. Where handbooks provide a higher level of due process, under the contract theory courts will require that students be provided with the procedural safeguards that have been promised.

Constitutional Substantive Due Process Rights. Rights traditionally considered as substantive include free speech, free press (rights of free speech and press are frequently combined as free expression), free exercise of religion, freedom of association, and privacy. Community college rules impinging on these substantive constitutional rights can be justified only if a sufficiently important interest of the college is represented in restricting student rights. For example, in *Orin v. Barclay* (2001), a community college permitted student protesters to conduct a prolife demonstration on the college quad with three stipulations: that they not cause a disturbance or breach of peace, that they not interfere with campus activities or access to campus buildings, and that they not engage in religious worship or instruction. The Tenth Circuit Court of Appeals upheld the first two stipulations because they were content-neutral and narrowly tailored to achieve the college's pedagogical interests. However, the court struck down the "no religion" stipulation as a content-based restriction that violated the students' religious speech rights. Under free speech, religious organizations have the same access to community college facilities as secular organizations do (*Widmar v. Vincent*, 1981).

Orin v. Barclay illustrates the principle that courts will scrutinize closely any restrictions that college officials impose on students' meeting for expressive purposes. When community college officials open facilities for student expression, their regulations about student use are limited to reasonable times (for example, certain hours of the day), places (for example, certain buildings or open areas on the campus), and manners of expression (for example, they cannot impede the movement of other students) (*Burbridge v. Sampson*, 1999). College regulations must be narrowly limited to significant college interests, such as prohibiting uses that violate criminal laws. Regulations that prescribe permissible speech may be struck down as being overly broad.

Federal Statutory Rights. Colleges receiving federal funds must comply with federal statutes in addition to protecting the contractual and constitutional rights of students. Among the most familiar of these statutes are Title IX of the Educational Amendments of 1972, prohibiting discrimination based on gender; Title VI of the Civil Rights Act of 1964, prohibiting discrimination based on race, color, or national origin; the Rehabilitation Act of 1973 (Section 504), prohibiting discrimination based on disability; and the Family Rights and Privacy Act of 1976 (FERPA), providing college students with right of access to their education records maintained by a college and limiting disclosure of those records without student consent.

Community colleges are also subject to statutes that are not connected to receiving federal funds, particularly Titles II and III of the Americans with Disabilities Act (ADA) of 1990. Title II prohibits disability discrimination in public entities, such as public colleges and universities, and Title III prohibits disability discrimination in places of public accommodation, such as private institutions of higher education.

With the exception of FERPA, all of these statutes permit damage claims by students for violations, as well as damage claims under Section 1983 of the Civil Rights Act of 1871. Section 1983 permits plaintiffs alleging violations of constitutional rights or violations of federal statutes to sue for damages or to seek injunctive relief, such as reinstatement or expunging of records. In addition, students can file separate claims under these statutes for hostile environment harassment.

Students are entitled to attend and participate in an educational setting that is free from discriminatory treatment. Decisions concerning academic or disciplinary misconduct that reflect differences in treatment based on any of the protected categories previously identified can result in damage awards to students, including punitive damages (*Tolbert v. Queens College,* 2001). For example, an African American student alleged a Title VI violation when his enrollment was dropped for failure to pay fees while some white students who had not paid the fees were permitted to continue attending classes (*Fuller v. Rayburn,* 1998). The court found that the student was entitled to reinstatement but not to damages because the Eleventh Amendment to the U.S. Constitution barred damage awards under Title VI. Although the student in *Fuller* was not interested in reinstatement, the case demonstrates the different remedies that can be at stake in a discrimination case. However, colleges can set and enforce neutral requirements without violating nondiscrimination laws. Thus an African American student who alleged race and gender discrimination could be dismissed from an academic program in which she had failed two qualifying examinations (*Middlebrooks v. University of Maryland,* 1997).

Section 504 and the ADA are different from the other federal statutes in that they require college officials to make reasonable accommodations for students with disabilities. As more students with disabilities graduate from high schools with services provided under the Individuals with Disabilities Education Act (IDEA) and Section 504, they may seek similar accommodations in higher education. However, a student who is provided with a reasonable academic accommodation and still performs unsatisfactorily will not prevail (*Darian v. University of Massachusetts Boston,* 1997). Although courts expect colleges to accommodate reasonable requests, such as more time on tests or the use of sign language interpreters, they have thus far deferred from interfering with academic governance issues that affect students with disabilities, such as prohibiting students from using alternative course substitutions (*Gluckenburger v. Boston University,* 1998) or excusing student plagiarism (*Childress v. Clement,* 1998).

In *Gonzaga University v. Doe* (2002), the U.S. Supreme Court held that students are not permitted to sue for damages when student education records are disclosed in violation of FERPA. However, lest community college officials become complacent about adhering to FERPA disclosure requirements, the student in the *Gonzaga University case* recovered $450,000 in damages for violations of state common law claims of defamation, invasion of privacy, and breach of contract.

Student Safety

Students are entitled to a reasonably safe campus environment (Cloud, 2002). Historically, courts were reluctant to find liability for colleges resulting from injury to students caused by the intervening criminal or intentional actions of others (*Hall v. Board of Supervisors Southern University,* 1981). However, the law has changed. In the much-publicized case of *Tarasoff v. Regents of University of California* (1976), the Supreme Court of California ruled that a person could be liable in damages to the estate of a murdered individual. In this case, a therapist who had received confidential information about his client's intention to kill Tatiana Tarasoff had a duty to warn her. The notion that a person could be liable for a breach of duty to warn despite the criminal intervening act of another person has opened the door to extend this duty to other situations. In *Peterson v. San Francisco Community College District* (1984), the California Supreme Court relied on *Tarasoff* in determining that a college had a duty to warn a female student, assaulted by a male student, that other assaults had occurred in the same area in the past.

The responsibility of community college officials for the safety of their students is tied to a duty to warn students about dangers to them, even when those dangers result from the criminal actions of third parties. Frequently, this duty to warn is based on past harmful acts toward students, as was the case in *Peterson,* but increasingly, courts are finding a duty to warn because students are considered to be business invitees (*Johnson v. State of Washington,* 1995; *Williams v. State of Louisiana,* 2001). An invitee is a person who is on the campus for the purpose of the business for which the college exists, namely, providing educational services. The duty owed to an invitee by a college is to protect against dangers that college personnel know of or could have known of through reasonable discovery (*Walton v. State of Colorado,* 1998). Students can claim that injuries resulting from such dangers are foreseeable and therefore a college would be expected to have implemented reasonable safety measures to protect them. Failure to take protective measures would constitute a breach of duty by the college and form the basis for a negligence claim.

Especially troublesome for colleges are students on campus whose past criminal (or alleged criminal) conduct is known. In *Nero v. Kansas State University* (1993), a state supreme court held that a female student, raped in a dormitory's basement laundry by a male student who had been indicted for the rape of another student three months earlier, could sue the university for negligence. University officials had permitted the male student to enroll for a summer intersession course while he was under indictment for the previous assault, placing him in a coed dorm where the plaintiff lived. In light of the facts in the case, the plaintiff was entitled to go to trial since knowing the male was a fellow dorm student "[gave] her a false sense of security" (p. 780). The court concluded that since the university had no obligation to accept the male student for the summer intersession, it should not have admitted him if the only campus housing available for the summer was a coed dorm.

On the other hand, New York's highest court reversed liability for a university that admitted a convicted felon who had served his sentence and who later raped and murdered a fellow student while attending the university. In balancing the benefits to the felon to pursue his education and the rights of other students to be free from harm, the court held that release of the felon to attend the university constituted a discretionary function giving the university immunity from a lawsuit and that the university had no duty to restrict the felon's activities on campus or warn other students (*Eiseman v. State of New York*, 1987). In a sweeping conclusion, the court observed that, at least in New York, "consistent with conditions of parole, an individual returned to freedom can frequent places of public accommodation, secure employment, and if qualified become a student" (p. 616).

Federal statutes and regulations since *Eiseman* suggest that college officials now probably have a duty to warn students about dangers, including dangerous persons, on or near campuses. In the Crime Awareness and Campus Security Act (1990), Congress required that colleges implement the following: policies concerning security and access to campus facilities, procedures for students and others to report crimes, programs to inform students about the prevention of crimes, and collection and reporting procedures for criminal offenses. The duty to report crimes applies to the campus and facilities owned by the college, as well as to public property (such as sidewalks, streets, or parking lots) that is in the reasonably contiguous area of the campus. The crimes that must be reported include criminal homicide, murder and nonnegligent manslaughter, negligent manslaughter, sex offenses (forcible or nonforcible), robbery, aggravated assault, burglary, motor vehicle theft, manslaughter, arson, and arrests of persons referred for disciplinary action involving liquor law violations, drug-related violations, and weapons possession (Code of Federal Regulations, Section 668.46(c), 2002). If a community college has more than one campus, the reporting must be done separately for each campus (Code of Federal Regulations, Section 668.46(d), 2002).

In 1994, Congress enacted the Campus Sex Crimes Prevention Act as part of the Violent Crime Control and Law Enforcement Act (1994), which took effect in 1996. The act states that sex offenders required to register under state law must report to an appropriate state agency, identifying any higher education institution in which they are employed or are enrolled as a student, as well as reporting changes in their status. Although this act does not require educational institutions to request the reported information from students, one can certainly argue that a recent U.S. Supreme Court decision has changed this perspective. In *Smith v. Doe* (2003), the Supreme Court upheld an Alaska state statute that required sex offenders to register and that placed their names on the Internet. *Smith v. Doe* would seem to have eliminated concern about the privacy rights of persons who are past sex offenders. Thus where information about specific sex offenders has been made public, colleges arguably have a duty to make students aware of offenders on the campus, but whether failure to make the information available will lead to damages awards if students are sexually assaulted remains to be seen.

Codes of Conduct

Given the trend in some states to include educational contracts under state consumer protection statutes, taking action against a student without providing adequate notice of a college's expectations and remedies could be considered a deceptive practice (*Alexson v. Hudson Valley Community College*, 2000). Even without such statutes, basic fairness demands that college publications include information about the conduct and well-being of students enrolled in the college. This information is usually presented in the form of codes of conduct that describe what the college expects of students.

Codes of conduct should be written clearly and enforced fairly. Colleges should identify the kinds of academic and disciplinary misconduct that could subject a student to punishment and encourage students to report misconduct to specifically identified college officials. When drafting procedures for handling rule violations, colleges should be aware that courts will overlay the college's procedures with due process requirements (*Trzop v. Centre College*, 2000). Among the due process rights that courts will expect are notice of charges, a fair hearing with unbiased adjudicators, an opportunity for the accused to respond by presenting evidence and cross-examining witnesses, and an appeal to a person or committee not involved in the dispute.

Students who are charged with violations of the student code are entitled to due process. Failure to provide minimum due process can result in the student's being reinstated and the awarding of damages (*Lee v. Board of Trustees of Western Illinois University*, 2000; *Cerussi v. Union College*, 2001). Especially troublesome for students is an understanding of the college's definition of, and punishment for, misconduct such as plagiarism, cheating, and hazing (Mawdsley, 1994; Guynn, 2002). If colleges intend to use degree revocation as a remedy for violations of rules not discovered until after the student has graduated (for example, that a student plagiarized papers or cheated on a test), the college needs to provide notice that revocation is a possible sanction for certain offenses (*Goodreau v. Rector and Visitors of the University of Virginia*, 2000).

Colleges should include safety policies and procedures in codes of conduct, identifying efforts that have been made to secure the campus: placement of physical barriers, location of alarm systems, campus call boxes, video cameras, well-lighted walk areas and parking lots, and location and phone number of campus-sponsored escort personnel (Cloud, 2002). To ensure that safety procedures are always current, colleges should have a student and faculty safety committee that meets regularly to address safety concerns. In addition, the college needs to engage a risk management consultant to perform a safety assessment of the campus and an attorney to prepare codes of conduct that are clearly understandable. Since most community college students attend part time, college officials should also arrange orientation sessions, especially regarding campus safety, during the evenings if many students would not be available during the day.

Conclusion

Community colleges, like other higher education institutions, must do more today than just deliver academic programs. Student safety, in the wake of the terrorist attacks of September 11, 2001, and the massacre at Columbine High in Colorado, has become a major concern for students and college personnel. Awareness of problem areas and problem students requires that colleges develop strategies for permitting students and college personnel to report their safety concerns. With reporting, though, comes a concomitant responsibility to investigate the reports, keeping in mind that the individuals being investigated will have due process rights. Failure to act in response to safety concerns can result in liability if a student or an employee is able to prove that action would have prevented an injury. Clearly, college officials have a delicate balancing act in protecting both safety and due process.

Primarily, though, students are on the campuses of community colleges because they are purchasing educational services. As such, they have a contractual right to have courses delivered as promised in catalogues, brochures, and syllabi. To the extent that state law recognizes students as consumers, students can recover damages for fraud or misrepresentation if the services delivered were not as advertised. Even though the number of student lawsuits for breach of contract or misrepresentation is relatively low, community college officials must be vigilant that the academic product being delivered is consistent with what was promised.

References

Cloud, R. C. "Safety on Campus." *Education Law Reporter,* 2002, *162,* 1–27.
Guynn, K. "Hazing in Public and Private High Schools: An Analysis of Legal Responses to Hazing." Unpublished dissertation, College of Education, Cleveland State University, 2002.
Mawdsley, R. D. *Academic Misconduct: Cheating and Plagiarism.* Dayton, Ohio: Education Law Association, 1994.

Legal References

Alexson v. Hudson Valley Community College, 125 F.Supp.2d 27 (N.D.N.Y. 2000).
Americans with Disabilities Act, 42 U.S.C. Section 12101 et seq. (1990).
Andre v. Pace University, 618 N.Y.S.2d 975 (City Ct. 1994).
Board of Curators of University of Missouri v. Horowitz, 435 U.S. 78 (1978).
Burbridge v. Sampson, 74 F.Supp.2d 940 (C.D.Cal. 1999).
Campus Sex Crimes Prevention Act, 42 U.S.C. 170101 (1994).

Cencor, Inc., v. Tolman, 868 P.2d 396 (Colo. 1994).
Cerussi v. Union College, 144 F.Supp.2d 265 (S.D.N.Y. 2001).
Childress v. Clement, 5 F.Supp.2d 384 (E.D.Va. 1998).
Civil Rights Act of 1871, 42 U.S.C. Section 1983.
Clayton v. Princeton University, 608 F.Supp. 413 (D.N.J. 1985).
Code of Federal Regulations, 34 C.F.R. Section 668.46(c) and (d), 2002.
Crime Awareness and Campus Security Act, 20 U.S.C. Section 1092 (1990).
Crook v. Baker, 813 F.2d 88 (6th Cir. 1987).
Darian v. University of Massachusetts Boston, 980 F.Supp. 77 (D.Mass. 1997).
Dezick v. Umpqua Community College, 599 P.2d 444 (Ore. 1979).
Dinu v. President and Fellows of Harvard College, 56 F.Supp.2d 129 (D.Mass. 1999).
Eiseman v. State of New York, 518 N.Y.S.2d 698 (N.Y. 1987).
Family Rights and Privacy Rights Act of 1976 (FERPA), 20 U.S.C. Section 1232g.
Fellheimer v. Middlebury College, 869 F. Supp. 238 (D.Vt. 1994).
Flannery v. Board of Trustees of Illinois Community College District No. 519, 196 WL 663918 (N.D.Ill. 1996).
Fuller v. Rayburn, 161 F.3d 516 (8th Cir. 1998).
Gluckenburger v. Boston University, 8 F.Supp.2d 82 (D.Mass. 1998).
Gonzaga University v. Doe, 536 U.S. 273 (2002).
Goodreau v. Rector and Visitors of the University of Virginia, 116 F.Supp.2d 694 (W.D. Va. 2000).
Hall v. Board of Supervisors Southern University, 405 So.2d 1125 (La.Ct.App. 1981).
Hall v. Medical College of Ohio at Toledo, 742 F.2d 299 (6th Cir. 1984).
Individuals with Disabilities in Education Act, 20 U.S.C. Section 1400 et seq. (1991).
Johnson v. State of Washington, 894 P.2d 1366 (Wash.Ct.App. 1995).
Lee v. Board of Trustees of Western Illinois University, 202 F.3d 274 (7th Cir. 2000).
Mangla v. Brown University, 135 F.3d 80 (1st Cir. 1991).
Middlebrooks v. University of Maryland, 980 F.Supp. 824 (D.Md. 1997).
Nero v. Kansas State University, 861 P.2d 768 (Kans. 1993).
Orin v. Barclay, 272 F.3d 1207 (10th Cir. 2001).
Peterson v. San Francisco Community College District, 205 Cal. Rptr. 842 (Cal. 1984).
Regents of University of Michigan v. Ewing, 474 U.S. 214 (1985).
Rehabilitation Act of 1973, 29 U.S.C. Section 794.
Ross v. Creighton University, 957 F.2d 410 (7th Cir. 1992).
Smith v. Doe, 123 S.Ct. 1140 (2003).
Susan M. v. New York Law School, 556 N.Y.S.2d 1104 (N.Y. 1990).
Tarasoff v. Regents of University of California, 131 Cal.Rptr. 14 (Cal. 1976).
Title VI, 42 U.S.C. Section 2000d (1964).
Title IX, 20 U.S.C. Section 1681 et seq. (1972).
Tolbert v. Queens College, 242 F.3d 58 (2d Cir. 2001).
Trahms v. Trustees of Columbia University in City of New York, 666 N.Y.S.2d 150 (N.Y.App.Div. 1997).
Troknya v. Cleveland Chiropractic Clinic, 280 F.3d 1200 (8th Cir. 2002).
Trzop v. Centre College, 2000 WL 1134505 (Ky.Ct.App. 2000).
Violent Crime Control and Law Enforcement Act, 42 U.S.C. 14071 (1994).
Walton v. State of Colorado, 968 P.2d 636 (Colo. 1998).
Widmar v. Vincent, 454 U.S. 263 (1981).
Williams v. State of Louisiana, 786 So.2d 927 (La.Ct.App. 2001).
Williams v. State University of New York, 674 N.Y.S.2d 702 (N.Y.App.Div. 1998).
Woodis v. Westark Community College, 160 F.3d 435 (8th Cir. 1998).

RALPH D. MAWDSLEY, J.D., *is professor of educational administration in the School of Education at Cleveland State University.*

2

Community colleges serve a higher percentage of students with disabilities than any other sector of higher education. An understanding of the requirements imposed by disability laws in accommodating those students is important for all community college leaders.

Accommodating Students with Disabilities

Constance S. Hawke

The profile of persons with disabilities has changed over the past decade. Traditionally, an individual with disabilities was likely to be older, poorer, unemployed, and less educated (Prentice, 2002). However, growing numbers of disabled persons are enrolling in postsecondary institutions. Recent statistics indicate that more than half a million disabled students are currently enrolled in higher education nationwide. Community colleges serve the largest segment of that population, enrolling up to 71 percent of all postsecondary students with disabilities (Barnett, 1996). Those numbers may be conservative, as many students with disabilities are not readily identified as disabled. At least one survey indicates that while approximately 8 percent of community college students reported a disability, only half that number requested an accommodation (Treloar, 1999).

Not only do community colleges serve a higher percentage of the disabled, but they also deal with a broader range of disabilities, often accommodating severely disabled students as well as older-than-average students (Gilpin, 1990). The most frequently mentioned disabilities among community college students are learning disabilities, mobility or orthopedic impairments, health impairments, mental illness, and emotional disturbance. Smaller percentages of students report hearing impairments, visual impairments, and speech or language impairments (National Center for Education Statistics, 1999).

The influx of students with disabilities into higher education has been fueled by passage of the Rehabilitation Act of 1973 and the Americans with Disabilities Act of 1990, both of which prohibit educational institutions from discriminating against disabled students. Prior to the enactment of these laws, few students with disabilities could overcome the many obstacles that precluded attending college. These barriers were not only physical (for example, inaccessible classrooms) but programmatic as well (inability to participate in traditional classroom instruction). Now postsecondary institutions must not only ensure that their buildings and facilities are accessible to the disabled but also, when necessary, provide a wide range of adaptive equipment, tutoring, alternative examination times and formats, counseling, taped texts, note-takers, interpreters, and accessible cyberspace applications. Disabled students attending community colleges are increasingly sophisticated about their legal rights. This generation is graduating from high school under the auspices of the Individuals with Disabilities in Education Act (IDEA), which guarantees a free and appropriate education for all disabled students in primary and secondary public education. Under IDEA, school districts are obligated to identify and evaluate students who may be in need of special education. Once identified, the student is entitled to an individualized education plan (IEP), regardless of the expense to the school district. Many of these students, and their parents, expect comparable treatment in the postsecondary environment, despite the fact that the same legal obligations do not exist. In recognition of increasing numbers of disabled students, the Office of Civil Rights (2002) within the U.S. Department of Education recently issued a publication to inform disabled students of what they should expect from postsecondary education institutions.

In light of the rising demand for accommodations and services on community college campuses, an understanding of the legal and regulatory requirements is important for administrators. This is true not only for those providing student disability services but also for administrators who are making decisions about procurement, budgets, and the campus environment—all of which are affected by disability discrimination laws.

The remainder of this chapter addresses major laws and supporting regulations that affect provisions for disability services, discusses what is required of the institution with respect to access and support for disabled students, and makes recommendations for accommodating students with disabilities on college campuses.

Fourteenth Amendment

Prior to the enactment of federal laws specifically prohibiting discrimination against persons with disabilities, the Fourteenth Amendment to the Constitution of the United States provided the legal basis for claims of disability discrimination. Under the amendment's equal protection clause, states may not deny equal protection under the law to persons within their jurisdiction. Since its ratification in 1868, the Fourteenth Amendment has been deemed to apply to all public entities, including postsecondary institutions.

Claims for disability discrimination brought under the equal protection clause are considered by the court pursuant to one of the standards of review established by the U.S. Supreme Court over time. Disability claims are subject to the "rational basis" test, the least intensive form of scrutiny a court can impose. In those cases, the disabled plaintiff has the legal burden of proving that the policy or practice of the institution has no rational or reasonable basis, a difficult task indeed.

Nevertheless, in cases where the actions of the college are clearly arbitrary, the disabled plaintiff may "attach" the Fourteenth Amendment claim to an action brought pursuant to Section 1983 of the Ku Klux Klan Act of 1871 (42 U.S.C. Section 1983). Section 1983 does not create any new rights for individuals, but, where an existing right has allegedly been violated (for example, equal protection), the statute permits the individual claiming the violation to file a lawsuit against individual administrators as well as against the institution. Moreover, Section 1983 allows for a broad range of remedies for the alleged wrong, including compensatory and punitive damages and reimbursement of attorneys' fees. Given the difficulty in prevailing on a Fourteenth Amendment and Section 1983 claim, most lawsuits claiming disability discrimination are based on the protections afforded under more recent federal laws.

Rehabilitation Act of 1973

Section 504 of the Rehabilitation Act of 1973 states that "no otherwise qualified individual with a disability. . . . shall, solely by reason of her or his disability, be excluded from participation in, be denied the benefits of, or be subjected to discrimination under any program receiving Federal financial assistance" (29 U.S. C. Section 794). Section 504 specifically covers postsecondary institutions, including colleges and universities that receive any kind of federal financial assistance, including student loans. In addition, if direct or indirect federal aid is received for *any* program or activity of the college, the institution is bound to comply with Section 504 requirements in *all* its programs and activities, whether they are federally subsidized or not (42 U.S.C. Section 2000d-4(a)(b)(A)). Virtually every postsecondary institution, public and private, receives federal dollars in some form and must therefore comply with Section 504.

Not only are institutions prohibited from discriminating against students (and employees) with disabilities under Section 504, but they are also obligated to provide reasonable accommodations for disabled students such that they do not merely participate in but also benefit from the program in which they are enrolled. Accordingly, Section 504 requires that the college provide equal access to admission, financial aid, employment assistance, and nonacademic services such as transportation and athletics. Under the regulations implementing the Rehabilitation Act (34 CFR Section 104), the college is responsible for ensuring compliance by appointing a coordinator to oversee and fulfill Section 504 requirements (34 CFR Section 104.7(a)). It is beyond the scope of this chapter to identify and discuss all of the federal regulations governing institutional compliance with Section 504 guidelines. For specific information on the regulations and the consequences for failure to comply, refer to the law itself (34 CFR Section 104).

Notwithstanding the mandates of Section 504 for admitting and accommodating "otherwise qualified" individuals with disabilities, the Supreme Court has made it clear that colleges do not have to change or lower admission standards simply because an applicant is disabled. Accordingly, a student must be able to meet the academic and technical requirements of the academic program if his or her disability is accommodated. For example, a college does not have to admit a hearing-impaired student to its nursing program if there is no reasonable accommodation that would enable the student to safely participate in the program (*Southeastern Community College v. Davis*, 1979). In another case, however, the Court held that there was no reason to deny an applicant with multiple sclerosis admission to a psychiatric residency solely on the basis of his disability (*Pushkin v. Regents of University of Colorado*, 1981). If a student can be successful in an academic or nonacademic program with a reasonable level of accommodation, Section 504 mandates that the student be permitted to participate.

Americans with Disabilities Act of 1990

Congress enacted the Americans with Disabilities Act (ADA) in 1990 to "provide a clear and comprehensive mandate for the elimination of discrimination against individuals with disabilities" (42 U.S.C. Section 12101(b)(2)). The ADA is indeed comprehensive, extending to employment, public accommodations, government services, and telecommunications. Specifically, Title II of the ADA prohibits public entities, including community colleges, from denying qualified individuals with disabilities participation in or benefit from the programs, services, or activities they provide or from discriminating against individuals based on their disabilities (42 U.S.C. Section 12131). Title III of the ADA extends its mandates to private entities that provide places of public accommodation (42 U.S.C. Section 12182(a)). Thus most private colleges are required to comply with Title III (42 U.S.C. Section 12181(7)(j)).

Definitions Under ADA. *Discrimination* is defined in the ADA as "a failure to make reasonable modifications in policies, practices, or procedures, when such modifications are necessary to afford such goods, services, facilities, privileges, advantages, or accommodations to individuals with disabilities, unless the entity can demonstrate that making such modifications would fundamentally alter the nature of such goods, services, privileges, advantages, or accommodations" (42 U.S.C. 12182(b)(2)(A)(ii)). Central to any determination of discrimination is the threshold question of whether a person is considered an "individual with a disability" within the meaning of the ADA: "Disability means, with respect to an individual, a physical or mental impairment that substantially limits one or more major life activities of such individual; a record of such impairment; or being regarded as having such an impairment" (28 CFR Section 35.104).

A physical impairment can be any physiological disorder or condition, cosmetic disfigurement, or anatomical loss affecting any system of the body, including the neurological, musculoskeletal, respiratory, sensory, cardiovascular, reproductive, digestive, genitourinary, hemic, lymphatic, and endocrine systems, or the skin. A mental impairment encompasses any mental or psychological disorder such as mental retardation, organic brain syndrome, emotional or mental illness, and specific learning disabilities (28 CFR Section 35.104). Noncontagious disorders (cerebral palsy, epilepsy, multiple sclerosis) and contagious diseases (HIV, tuberculosis) are included within the definition of impairments, as are drug addiction and alcoholism. In each instance, the impairment must be one that substantially limits one or more major life activities, such as walking, breathing, hearing, seeing, or learning (28 CFR Section 35.104). To qualify as "substantially limited," the person must be unable to perform the activity or be significantly restricted in doing so (28 CFR Section 35, App. A).

Physical or mental impairment does not include homosexuality or bisexuality, nor do temporary conditions (such as a respiratory virus or broken limb) fall within the definition (28 CFR Section 35, App. A). Moreover, the ADA expressly excludes the following conditions from protection: transvestism, transsexualism, pedophilia, exhibitionism, compulsive gambling, kleptomania, pyromania, and substance abuse disorders resulting from current use of illegal drugs (28 CFR Section 35.104).

A person may also qualify for protection under the ADA if he or she has a record of impairment (for example, a history of treatment for tuberculosis, cancer, psychiatric disorder, or substance abuse). The ADA also addresses "perceived impairments" for individuals who are not actually impaired but are treated as disabled. For example, persons who are HIV-positive, burn victims with severe scarring, or persons with seizure disorders may not be treated discriminatorily (28 CFR Section 35.104, App. A).

Like Section 504, the ADA does not require an entity to provide a requested accommodation if its provision would result in a fundamental alteration to a program or activity or the accommodation would create an "undue hardship" for the institution. The ADA indicates that what constitutes an undue hardship is based on a number of factors, including the size and budget of the program, the number of employees of the institution, the type and cost of accommodation, the type of facility and operation, the availability of funding, and the impact on the employer's ability to conduct business (42 U.S.C. Section 12111(10); 29 CFR Section 1630.2(p)). Based on those factors, the college may claim undue hardship, but the courts may overrule the claim. In one case, for example, an institution determined that a requested accommodation for an employee's respiratory disability—the installation of an air purification system for an entire building—would create an undue hardship. The court disagreed in light of the university's total budget and required the installation (*Kent State University v. Ohio Civil Rights Commission,* 1989).

Web Accessibility. The ADA expressly requires public entities to ensure that communications with applicants, participants, and members of the public with disabilities are as effective as communications with others (28 CFR Section 35.160). Although neither the statute nor regulations expressly include the Web sites of public entities, both the Department of Education (DOE) and the Department of Justice (DOJ) have opined that Title II applies. Several years ago, the Department of Education responded to complaints against San Jose State University and the California community college system alleging that their Internet resources were not accessible to persons with visual impairments. The letter issued by the department indicated that the institutions could not simply respond to a request for accommodation on an ad hoc basis; the ADA creates an affirmative duty to establish comprehensive services. For example, the Office of Civil Rights (OCR) suggested that adaptive software should be provided to make computer information accessible, instead of providing the disabled individual with an assistive device such as a personal reader attendant (Shelton, 1996).

In addition, the DOE has interpreted Section 508 of the Rehabilitation Act—which expands requirements for access to the federal government's electronic and information technology—to apply to postsecondary institutions in states that receive federal funds under the Assistive Technology Act. Under Section 508, the scope of electronic and information technology includes computers (hardware, software, and data), facsimile machines, copiers, information transaction machines, telephones, and other equipment used for transmitting, receiving, or storing information (Foster, 2001).

In effect, ADA regulations and Section 504 are coextensive: a violation of one will constitute a violation of the other, and the analysis of the rights and obligations created by these disability laws is the same (*Zukle v. Regents of the University of California,* 1999). Both laws seek to eliminate unfair burdens for disabled students, not to provide them with benefits because of their disabilities (Cloud, 2000).

Implications for Community Colleges

Taken together, Section 504 and the ADA and their supporting regulations provide a framework for compliance. Within that framework, community colleges must take a comprehensive view of how they ensure equal access and support of students with disabilities, both on and off campus.

Technical Requirements. In conducting compliance assessment, it is recommended that the technical requirements of federal law be addressed first. Each college must have an individual identified to oversee compliance and address complaints. The establishment of grievance policies and procedures is critical. Colleges must publish a notice of nondiscrimination in their catalogues and other relevant materials (Washington University, 3 National Disability L. Rep. 327, OCR 1992).

Federal regulations also require the college administration to ensure the physical accessibility of buildings and facilities that are used by students, including classrooms and recreational facilities. This does not mean that every part of every building must be usable by the disabled. If the college wants to avoid the cost of making a building accessible, programs or activities should be relocated to another building that is accessible. If construction or renovation is necessary, specific guidelines detail everything from entrance ramps to the height of drinking fountains (Uniform Federal Accessibility Standards, 41 CFR Part 101–19.6, App. A; ADA Accessibility Guidelines for Buildings and Facilities, 28 CFR Part 36, App. A).

Since community colleges do not often provide housing for students, residence hall accessibility is not generally a concern; however, ensuring the appropriate accessibility of parking lots and garages is important to colleges with large commuter populations. Federal regulations determine the number, size, and location of parking spaces for the disabled. Students seeking permits for those parking spaces cannot be charged more than students obtaining a regular parking permit. If the college operates a transportation system, it must be accessible to students with disabilities, or an alternative system (such as special lift-equipped vans) must be operated to provide comparable services.

If a complaint is lodged with the DOE, the agency will investigate and render findings with respect to the alleged discriminatory activity. If a finding is made in favor of the complainant, the DOE will work with the institution to achieve voluntary compliance. Where the college refuses to comply, the U.S. attorney general may institute action against the college, possibly seeking injunctive relief and civil penalties up to $100,000 (42 U.S.C. Section 1288(b)(2)). At any time in the administrative process, the complainant may file suit in federal court (28 CFR Section 35.172(b)). ADA regulations specifically state that Eleventh Amendment immunity is not available as a defense to a lawsuit brought under Title II; accordingly, a college may be required to pay monetary damages where ADA violations are found (28 CFR Section 35.178). The ADA was amended in 1991 to permit a disabled plaintiff to seek compensatory and punitive damages at a jury trial and to recover attorneys' fees and expenses (Civil Rights Act of 1991, Pub. L. No. 102–166).

Although the need for physical accessibility has been addressed in recent decades, accessibility of electronic and information technology is relatively a new endeavor for college administrators (Hawke and Jannarone, 2002). Nevertheless, procurers of computer and electronic equipment now need to contemplate the use of that equipment by disabled students and employees. Although no formal decision has been made as to their applicability to postsecondary education, the Section 508 regulations (36 CFR

Section 1194) provide some standards that colleges may use in purchasing telecommunications, multimedia, and computer equipment. Colleges should also assess their existing Web pages to ensure that they are accessible to individuals with visual and auditory impairments (for example, pictures and auditory messages should have text alternatives that are available via a mouse click). Software packages can be purchased to aid in evaluating existing Web pages, and administrators should ensure that all college Web pages meet accessibility standards.

Admissions and Financial Aid. Educational institutions may not consider an applicant's disability when making admissions decisions. Equitable distribution of financial aid is often a challenge because of the large number of qualified applicants. In both admissions and financial aid determinations, the criteria for selection may not screen out individuals with disabilities unless those criteria are prerequisites for participating in the program. Once established, those criteria should be used for all applicants (East Central Community College, 4 National Disability L. Rep. 225, OCR 1993). If an applicant is qualified for admission using established criteria, he or she should be admitted, regardless of disability.

Requests for Accommodations. Contrary to the requirements of the IDEA for students in primary and secondary education, it is the responsibility of the postsecondary student to request accommodation for a disability. There is no obligation under federal law for a postsecondary institution to identify or otherwise seek out a student in need of accommodations. The claimed impairment must be one that is identified as a disability under Section 504 and the ADA (Thomas, 2002). For instance, test anxiety does not constitute a disability under federal law (*McGuiness v. University of New Mexico School of Medicine*, 1998). Moreover, the disability must substantially restrict a major life activity (Davidson County Community College, 6 National Disability L. Rep. 232, OCR 1994).

The appropriate medical professional should document the existence of a disability and provide recommendations for accommodations (Community College of Vermont, 4 National Disability L. Rep. 406, OCR 1993). The burden is on the student to provide sufficient documentation (Anne Arundel Community College, 13 National Disability L. Rep. 62, OCR 1998) and to do so in a time frame that allows the college to respond to the request.

Providing Accommodations. Once a request for accommodation has been made and supported by appropriate documentation, the college must decide if the accommodation is reasonable under the circumstances. Reasonable accommodations can include modifications to programs such as substitution of a required course, changes in delivery of instruction (for example, videotape or via the Internet), extension of time or format for examinations, and extensions of time to complete program requirements. Colleges may also need to provide auxiliary aids to individuals based on their needs, whether in the form of personnel (interpreters, note-takers, and transcribers) or assistive devices (listening devices, tape recorders, and closed captioning).

It is important to note that the educational institution does not have to grant every accommodation requested. As discussed earlier, neither the ADA nor Section 504 requires that the college fundamentally alter a program to make an accommodation (*Southeastern Community College v. Davis*, 1979). For an accommodation to constitute a fundamental alteration, it must be far more than a modification to the program—it has to compromise the essential nature of the program (*Alexander v. Choate*, 1985).

Nor does the institution have an obligation to engage in a single accommodation that is so excessive that it creates an undue hardship on the institution. Some specialized devices cost more than $5,000—and individuals may require multiple devices. However, caution should be exercised in citing cost as the sole determinant for denying a request for accommodation. In accordance with the regulations, the cost of the accommodation alone is not sufficient to withhold compliance, but a decision must take into consideration the size of the institution's budget, number of employees, and other factors. Although the institution should give deference to the recommendations of medical and other professionals familiar with a student's disability, it may deviate from those recommendations if suitable alternatives are available. Federal law does not create a legal right to all accommodations beneficial to a disabled student—only reasonable accommodations are required (*Hoffman v. Contra Costa College*, 2001). Consistent with the notion of reasonableness, there is no statutory requirement that the college explore every available alternative accommodation, unless it chooses to do so. It is the student who is charged with the responsibility for providing that information to the college (Massachusetts College of Pharmacy, 1 National Disability L. Rep. 369, OCR 1991). Indeed, there is some risk in deviating from the proposed request of a disabled adult and substituting an administrator's judgment. The Supreme Court has stated that there is no place for that kind of "paternalistic" authority in higher education (*Wright v. Columbia University*, 1981). In some instances, it is possible that no suitable accommodation can be made, based on the nature of the disability (Lewis and Clark College, 5 National Disability L. Rep. 248, OCR 1994).

Most requests for accommodation at community colleges will be of an obvious and routine nature, with no legal or financial analysis required. Deference should be given to the wishes of the student and the opinions of the professional who provides the supporting documentation. However, when the requests for accommodations require excessive or expensive adjustments, the decision-making process should be deliberate and involve legal and business counsel.

Conclusion

Postsecondary students are reporting disabilities and requesting accommodations in ever-increasing numbers. Community colleges are enrolling the greatest percentages of this population. The laws that are enacted to protect individuals with disabilities—Section 504 and the ADA—are intended to ensure equal educational opportunity and to eliminate unfair burdens on disabled students, not to give them any special benefits because of their disability (*Berg v. Florida Department of Labor and Employment*, 1998). Simply put, these laws attempt to "level the playing field" so that disabled students can participate equally in postsecondary education.

An understanding of the breadth and scope of these laws is essential for all community college administrators. For example, administrators charged with budgeting and procurement should consider the ongoing costs of providing accommodations and plan accordingly. Those responsible for campus facilities should be concerned about compliance with regulations for parking and physical accessibility. In an era of diminishing government support and scarce resources, community colleges may want to learn more about financial assistance that is available at the local, state, or federal level to support services for the disabled.

References

Barnett, L. (ed.). *Directory of Disability Support Services in Community Colleges.* Washington, D.C.: American Association of Community Colleges, 1996.

Cloud, R. C. "Higher Education Accommodations for Disabled Students." *West's Education Law Reporter*, 2000, *147*, 391–411.

Foster, A. "Making Web Sites Work for People with Disabilities." *Chronicle of Higher Education*, Feb. 2, 2001, p. A30.

Gilpin, B. "Identifying the Hidden Handicaps of the Older-Than-Average Student." Paper presented at the Building Foundations for Cultural Diversity conference, Costa Mesa, Calif., Jan. 25–27, 1990. (ED382229)

Hawke, C. S., and Jannarone, A. "Emerging Issues of Web Accessibility: Implications for Higher Education." *West's Education Law Reporter*, 2002, *160*(3), 715–727.

National Center for Education Statistics. *An Institutional Perspective on Students with Disabilities in Postsecondary Education.* Washington, D.C.: U.S. Department of Education, 1999.

Office of Civil Rights. *Students with Disabilities Preparing for Postsecondary Education: Know Your Rights and Responsibilities.* Washington, D.C.: U.S. Department of Education, 2002.

Prentice, M. *Serving Students with Disabilities at the Community College.* Washington, D.C.: Office of Educational Research and Improvement, 2002. (ED467984)

Shelton, P. G. (Team Leader, Compliance Division, U.S. Department of Education, Office for Civil Rights). Letter to Dr. Robert Caret, President, San Jose University, Jan. 25, 1996. [http://www.icdri.org/legal/sjsu.htm]. Accessed Jan. 17, 2004.

Thomas, S. B. *Students, Colleges, and Disability Law.* Dayton, Ohio: Education Law Association, 2002.

Treloar, L. L. "Editor's Choice: Lessons on Disability and the Rights of Students." *Community College Review*, 1999, *27*(1), 30–40.

Legal References

Alexander v. Choate, 469 U.S. 287, 298, 1985.

Berg v. Florida Department of Labor and Employment, Division of Vocational Rehabilitation, 163 F.3d 1251 (11th Cir. 1998).

Hoffman v. Contra Costa College, 2110 U.S. App. LEXIS 24398 (9th Cir. 2001).

Kent State University v. Ohio Civil Rights Commission, 581 N.E.2d 1135 (Ohio 1989).

McGuiness v. University of New Mexico School of Medicine, 170 F.3d 974 (10th Cir. 1998).

Pushkin v. Regents of University of Colorado, 658 F.2d 1372 (10th Cir. 1981).

Southeastern Community College v. Davis, 442 U.S. 397 (1979).

Wright v. Columbia University, 520 F.Supp. 789 (E.D. Pa 1981).

Zukle v. Regents of the University of California, 166 F.3d 1041 (9th Cir. 1999).

CONSTANCE S. HAWKE, J.D., *is associate legal counsel and the director of federal relations at Kent State University in Ohio. She is the author of* Computer and Internet Use on Campus: A Legal Guide to Issues of Intellectual Property, Free Speech, and Privacy *(Jossey-Bass, 2000).*

3

Discrimination, affirmative action, and evaluation are
legal issues that involve community college leadership.
Prudent leaders must cultivate the required legal
knowledge of these and other employment issues if they
are to lead effectively.

Employment Issues in the Community College

Todd A. DeMitchell

Education is a people-intensive enterprise. This is particularly true of community colleges. The primary responsibility of community college faculty is teaching rather than research or scholarly inquiry, and "instruction is stubbornly labor intensive" (Cohen and Brawer, 2003, p. 410). Therefore, the organizational efforts to recruit, retain, and when appropriate remove employees are critical to the success of the community college.

This chapter explores the major legal parameters that influence the administration of employment issues. The federal laws discussed are broadly based but clearly apply to community colleges, among other institutions. Some states provide more protection for individuals than federal law, and community college leaders are encouraged to review the pertinent laws in force in their state. And because litigation often involves a mix of state and federal claims, knowledge of specific state laws is necessary for administrators making employment decisions.

This chapter examines four aspects of employment issues in community colleges: federal discrimination statutes, affirmative action, performance evaluation, and considerations for effective employment policies, practices, and attitudes.

Federal Antidiscrimination Legislation

Brown v. Board of Education of Topeka (1954) is one of the landmark U.S. Supreme Court decisions that helped define public education in the latter half of the twentieth century. The Supreme Court recognized that educating African American children separately, even if done in "equal" facilities,

NEW DIRECTIONS FOR COMMUNITY COLLEGES, no. 125, Spring 2004   © Wiley Periodicals, Inc.

was inherently unequal because of the stigma attached to being educated separately through the force of law and because of the deprivation of some of the benefits that minorities would achieve in a racially integrated school system. The Supreme Court acknowledged that education is the most important function of state and local governments and the foundation of good citizenship, because it is the principal instrument of enculturation and preparation for later professional training. From this premise the Court argued, "It is doubtful that any child may reasonably be expected to succeed in life if he is denied the opportunity of an education. Such an opportunity, where the state has undertaken to provide it, is a right which must be made available to all on equal terms" (p. 493).

In addition to altering the landscape of public education, *Brown* provided the backdrop for the civil rights movement, a major goal of which was to rid the nation of the vestiges of discrimination. Since the 1960s, civil rights legislation has targeted discrimination based on race, color, national origin, religion, gender, and age. Legislation targeting discrimination against individuals with disabilities has more recently joined the arsenal of civil rights protections, thanks to Section 504 of the Rehabilitation Act of 1973 and the Americans with Disabilities Act.

Coupled with the deeply held American values of fair laws (substantive due process) and fair play (procedural due process), the laws against discrimination provide an important context for the employment procedures and attitudes for community college leaders. Although this chapter will provide a brief overview of the major discrimination protections, this legal knowledge must be infused with an attitude regarding the basic worth and dignity of applicants and employees. It is one's attitude that breathes life into statutory protections and moves them from form to substance.

Disparate Treatment and Disparate Impact. Title VII of the Civil Rights Act of 1964 (42 U.S.C. Section 2000e et seq.) is the most comprehensive and most frequently used federal discrimination law (Kaplin and Lee, 1995). It declares that it is unlawful for an employer to discriminate against an individual on the basis of race, color, religion, sex, or national origin. The legislation applies to both public community colleges and private two-year institutions with more than fifteen employees.

Title VII claims fall into two categories, disparate treatment and disparate impact. Disparate treatment is the more commonly litigated of the two. It is used when an individual alleges that he or she has been discriminated against in hiring, promotion, salary, or other benefit of employment.

The disparate treatment test was articulated by the U.S. Supreme Court in *McDonnell Douglas Corporation v. Green* (1973) and involves three steps. First, the plaintiff must establish that he or she is covered by Title VII (an easy fact to establish because Title VII protects both genders and all races, religions, and ethnic backgrounds); that the plaintiff applied for a position for which he or she was qualified; that despite the qualifications, the plaintiff was rejected; and that the employer continued to seek applicants who possessed the plaintiff's qualifications. Second, the employer must articulate legitimate, nondiscriminatory reasons for the hiring decision. For example, in *Lewis v. Chattahoochee Valley Community College* (2001), the college asserted that the dismissal of an African American female professor was not based on her race or gender but was due to financial concerns, a legitimate, nondiscriminatory reason. Third, the plaintiff must demonstrate that the nondiscriminatory reasons proffered by the employer were a pretext for discrimination.

For example, in *La Fleur v. Wallace State Community College* (1996), the female African American plaintiff successfully rebutted the college's assertion that the adverse employment decision was based, in part, on her academic credentials. She asserted that the reason was a mere pretext for discrimination because a master's degree was required for the position, not a doctorate, and that her immediate supervisor had made discriminatory and race-based threats.

Disparate impact cases assert that an apparently nondiscriminatory employment policy has a discriminatory impact on a class of persons protected by Title VII. In *Griggs v. Duke Power Company* (1971), the Supreme Court wrote, "Practice, procedures, or tests neutral on their face, and even neutral in terms of intent, cannot be maintained if they operate to 'freeze' the status quo of prior discriminatory practices" (p. 429). Courts typically review the cumulative impact of the employment practice under review and then shift the burden to the defendant employer to articulate a "business justification" for the practice.

Sexual Harassment. Title VII protects individuals from unwelcome sexual advances, requests for sexual favors, and other verbal and physical conduct of a sexual nature in the workplace. The first type of sexual harassment is categorized as *quid pro quo*. This kind of harassment usually involves expressed or implied demands for sex in exchange for job benefits. The classic example is the supervisor who tells his or her subordinate that to continue working, she or he must submit to the supervisor's sexual demands. "In its most basic form, it is sex for employment—*quid pro quo*" (DeMitchell, 1994, p. 221).

The second category of sexual harassment is the hostile environment. A hostile environment claim usually involves a continuing or severe violation. Typically, the plaintiff must show that "the acts of defendant 'rise to the level of a dogged pattern' of discrimination as distinguished from 'isolated and sporadic outbreaks'" (*Purrington v. University of Utah*, 1993, p. 1028). This category is more difficult to identify than quid pro quo harassment. In *Meritor Savings Bank v. Vinson* (1986), the Supreme Court confirmed that a hostile environment violates Title VII: "Sexual harassment which creates a hostile environment or offensive environment for members of one sex is every bit the arbitrary barrier to sexual equality at the workplace that racial harassment is to racial equality. Surely, a requirement that a man or woman run a gauntlet of sexual abuse in return for the privilege of being allowed to work and make a living can be demeaning and disconcerting as the harshest racial epithets" (p. 2406, quoting *Henson v. Dundee,* 1982).

Not all questions were answered by the *Meritor* decision. In 1993, the Supreme Court decided another hostile environment case (*Harris v. Forklift Systems, Inc.,* 1993) and articulated the following standard of review (pp. 370–371):

1. The conduct must be severe or pervasive enough to create an objectively hostile environment.
2. A reasonable person would find the environment hostile.
3. The victim perceives the environment as hostile.
4. Whether an environment is hostile is determined by looking at all the circumstances. These circumstances may include the frequency of the discriminatory conduct, its severity, whether it is physically threatening or humiliating or a merely offensive utterance, and whether it unreasonably interferes with an employee's work performance.

Title VII discrimination in the workplace is applicable to supervisor actions toward subordinates, coworker actions creating a hostile environment, and same-sex harassment (*Oncale v. Sundowner Offshore Services, Inc.,* 1998).

Sexual Orientation Discrimination. An evolving and contentious social issue is the extension of legal protection for discrimination based on sexual orientation. For example, in an equal protection case involving the harassment of a gay student, the Seventh Circuit Court of Appeals wrote: "The gravamen of equal protection lies not in the fact of deprivation of a right but in the invidious classification of persons aggrieved by a state's actions. A plaintiff must demonstrate intentional or purposeful discrimination to show an equal protection violation" (*Nabozny v. Podlesny,* 1996, p. 453). Therefore, a showing of mere negligence will not suffice to support charges of discrimination based on sexual orientation.

An equal protection analysis involves the use of one of three tests. The first test is strict scrutiny analysis, which gives the least deference to governmental action. Classifications based on race always trigger the use of strict scrutiny analysis and come to the courts with a heavy presumption against their validity. The middle tier or heightened scrutiny is used when the classification is based on gender or national origin. However, the Supreme Court in *Romer v. Evans* (1996) held that classifications based on sexual orientation are judged using the most deferential test to government, rational basis. This test requires that governmental action be rationally related to a legitimate state interest.

For example, a schoolteacher brought suit against his school district alleging that that the school district treated him differently when addressing complaints based solely on discrimination he suffered in relation to his homosexuality (*Schroeder v. Hamilton School District,* 2002). The plaintiff asserted that he was discriminated against because of his sexual orientation in violation of the equal protection clause of the Fourteenth Amendment and 42 U.S.C. Section 1983. The majority of the court of appeals held that the school district's responses to the plaintiff's complaints were not irrational. Thus the school district passed the rational basis test and was found not to have violated the equal protection clause. The court also asserted that Title VII, discussed earlier, does not "provide a private right of action based on sexual orientation discrimination" (p. 951).

Individuals alleging discrimination based on their sexual orientation may seek redress through state courts for violations of state discrimination laws. Or plaintiffs may access the federal courts by way of an equal protection cause of action. The use of either avenue makes clear that complaints of harassment based on sexual orientation must be investigated and that reasonable steps must be taken to end the harassment.

Age Discrimination. The Age Discrimination in Employment Act (ADEA; 29 U.S.C. Section 621 et seq.) provides protection from discrimination based on age. Enacted in 1967, the ADEA makes it unlawful for an employer to discriminate against a person who is forty years of age or older in any employment decision such as hiring, promotion, discharge, compensation, and terms, conditions, and privileges of employment. In 1978, the ADEA was amended and the mandatory retirement age of sixty-five was increased to age seventy. In 1986, it was uncapped, with two exceptions. The first exception pertained to individuals in public safety positions, such as firefighters and police officers. The second exception was for high-level policymakers and tenured faculty members in higher education. In 1994, the mandatory retirement age for faculty was abolished.

The adjudication of ADEA complaints employs the same two tests of disparate treatment and disparate impact used in Title VII employment issues. For example, Hendrickson (1999) noted that in *Fisher v. Asheville-Buncombe Technical Community College* (1993), a faculty member sued for age discrimination under disparate treatment. The institution provided a valid reason for the nonrenewal of the contract (poor performance by way of refusal to adapt to new curricular changes), and the plaintiff was unable to demonstrate that the offered reasons were merely a pretext.

Discrimination Against Employees with Disabilities. Chapter Two includes a detailed analysis of the two major federal laws protecting the rights of community college students with disabilities. The Rehabilitation Act of 1973 and the Americans with Disabilities Act of 1990 also apply to community college employees. Section 504 of the Rehabilitation Act of 1973 provides in pertinent part that no "otherwise qualified individual with a disability . . . shall . . . be excluded from participation in, be denied the benefits of, or be subjected to discrimination under any program or activity receiving Federal financial assistance" (29 U.S.C. Section 794(a)).

Section 504 is a civil rights statute. It is the analog for the disabled of the Civil Rights Act of 1964 (Yudof, Kirp, and Levin, 1992). Compliance with Section 504 provisions is monitored by the U.S. Department of Education's Office for Civil Rights (OCR). Employees may file complaints directly with OCR, which is obligated to investigate and to take appropriate action. Once OCR investigates a complaint, it is not required to limit its investigation to the particulars of the complaint. It may conduct a compliance review that looks into every aspect of the way a community college meets its Section 504 obligations to employees. Unlike special education legislation (Individuals with Disabilities Act, 20 U.S.C. Section 1400), Section 504 does not provide any funds to defray the costs of ensuring nondiscrimination.

There are two provisions that must be met in order for an employee to qualify for Section 504 protections and services. The employee must be disabled within the meaning of the statute and must be "qualified, or otherwise qualified" (see Chapter Two). Otherwise qualified individuals are those "who could meet all the program admission requirements in spite of their handicap" (*Southeastern Community College v. Davis*, 1979, p. 406). Community colleges are required to make reasonable accommodations for "otherwise qualified" employees with disabilities. However, the community college need not alter essential performance requirements of the position to meet the needs of an otherwise qualified employee. Furthermore, the cost of the accommodation may be considered in assessing the reasonableness of the accommodation for the disability (*Alexander v. Choate*, 1985). For example, a reasonable accommodation might require the college to eliminate unnecessary job qualifications or restructure physical access in work areas. Finally, an employee with a disability recognized under Section 504 is not entitled to special protections and may be disciplined for misconduct that is not a result of his or her disability.

The Americans with Disabilities Act (ADA; 42 U.S.C. Section 12101 et seq.) was enacted in 1990, but the "number of professors who have successfully brought ADA actions is slight" (Abram, 2003, p. 11). Employees in ADA cases face two hurdles. First, the employee must demonstrate that he or she has a disability that substantially limits a major life function. Second, a reasonable accommodation must enable the person to be an otherwise qualified individual. The disability and the resulting reasonable accommodation must allow the employee to perform the essential functions of the job.

For example, in *Horton v. Board of Trustees of Community College District No. 508* (1997), a professor's ADA claim that an unspecified nervous disorder caused him to miss teaching his classes failed. The essential functions of a community college professor are to prepare for and teach classes. Therefore, an inability to teach classes precludes any reasonable accommodation. Similarly, in *Motzkin v. Trustees of Boston University* (1996), a professor claimed that he was disabled because he could not refrain from sexually harassing women. The court accepted his disability but held that the disability was so severe that he was not an otherwise qualified individual.

Affirmative Action

Affirmative action plans are enacted to provide equal protection and equal access to groups that have historically suffered the injustices and the indignities of discrimination. Although these plans seek to provide a remedy to discrimination based on race or gender, they have been attacked and dismantled because they discriminate on the basis of race and gender. On occasion, individuals (usually white and often male) who believe that employment affirmative action plans have discriminated against them have used Title VII to seek legal remedy for "reverse discrimination."

Michigan Cases. Recently, the U.S. Supreme Court decided two cases related to the University of Michigan, one involving undergraduate admission (*Gratz v. Bollinger,* 2003) and the other concerning admission to the law school (*Grutter v. Bollinger,* 2003). Although these two cases do not specifically address employment affirmative action programs, they are instructive.

Both cases involved a white applicant who was denied admission and brought suit alleging discrimination based on race. Chief Justice William Rehnquist, writing for the majority in *Gratz v. Bollinger,* held that the admissions policy of distributing 20 points, or one-fifth of the points needed for admission, on the basis of membership in a specific underrepresented minority defined by race violated the equal protection clause of the Fourteenth Amendment. Justice Sandra O'Connor, in her concurring opinion, was persuaded to find the policy constitutionally infirm in part because the system was nonindividualized and mechanical (p. 2433).

However, in *Grutter v. Bollinger,* the Supreme Court upheld the law school admissions policy in a 5-to-4 decision. The Court argued that "universities occupy a special niche in our constitutional tradition" (p. 2339) and gave deference to the university's definition of diversity as a compelling interest. It is unknown if a community college's pursuit of diversity would be accorded the same status of a special niche in our constitutional framework as universities receive. In addition to holding that diversity represents a compelling state interest and is constitutionally legitimate, Justice O'Connor's majority opinion for the first time designated a sunset date for affirmative action plans. She wrote, "We expect that 25 years from now, the use of racial preferences will no longer be necessary to further the interest approved today" (p. 2347). Keeping an eye on the calendar may be prudent for admissions and human resource officials.

Layoffs and Affirmative Action. In 1972, the Jackson Board of Education in Michigan responded to the racial tension in the community by voluntarily negotiating an affirmative action layoff agreement with its teachers' union that would protect employees who were minorities against layoffs. In 1974, layoffs became necessary, but the board refused to implement the layoff article when it became apparent that tenured white teachers would be laid off and nontenured minority teachers would be retained. The union with two laid-off minority teachers brought suit in federal court, alleging a violation of the equal protection clause. The court rejected the board's argument that the layoff provision violated the Civil Rights Act of 1964.

After the judgment, the board adhered to the provision resulting in nonminority teachers' being laid off while minority teachers with less seniority were retained. The displaced nonminority teachers brought suit in federal court, alleging violations of the equal protection clause, Title VII, and 42 U.S.C Section 1983. The court ruled against the plaintiffs, finding that racial preferences were permissible under the equal protection clause as an attempt to remedy societal discrimination by providing "role models" for minority schoolchildren.

The Court of Appeals for the Sixth Circuit agreed, largely adopting the language and reasoning of the lower court. Neither court used strict scrutiny analysis. The Supreme Court granted review only on the equal protection clause claim. Strict scrutiny analysis was used because the negotiated layoff provision operated "against whites and in favor of certain minorities, and therefore constitutes a classification based on race." The Supreme Court, on a vote of 5 to 4, reversed the Court of Appeals for the Sixth Circuit (*Wygant v. Jackson Board of Education*, 1986).

Five separate opinions were written, demonstrating the fractured view of affirmative action programs when race is a criterion. Justice Lewis Powell wrote the plurality opinion, arguing that societal discrimination without a showing of specific discrimination was too "amorphous" a basis for imposing a racially classified remedy. In other words, a specific defendant can be held responsible only for discrimination caused by that defendant rather than for discrimination generally present in society. Furthermore, Justice Powell argued that the role model theory advanced by the district court was a double-edged sword. One edge could be used to justify a small percentage of minority teachers by reference to a small percentage of black students. The opposite edge of the role model theory—that black students are better off with black teachers—when carried to its logical conclusion, Justice Powell asserted, could lead to the very system rejected in *Brown v. Board of Education* in 1954.

According to *Wygant v. Jackson,* several conditions must exist for affirmative action employment plans to survive strict scrutiny. In cases where affirmative action plans involve hiring goals, "the burden [of achieving racial equality] to be borne by innocent individuals is diffused to a considerable extent among society generally" rather than imposed on particular individuals (p.1851). The *Wygant* decision also sharply limited the "ability of public institutions to use race- or gender-conscious hiring or promotion policies to redress historical imbalance unless there is clear evidence of discrimination" (Kaplin and Lee, 1995, p. 270).

Performance Evaluation

As stated at the beginning of the chapter, the important work of the community college gets done through and by individuals. Fair regulations (substantive due process) and fair procedures (procedural due process) are the foundation of an evaluation system. A fair system of evaluation provides stability for employees. Stability allows for growth. Uncertainty leads to reduced effectiveness. The following critical questions regarding employee evaluations must be addressed.

- *What* will be evaluated—what standards for performance will be used?
- *How* shall the evaluation be conducted—will fairness suffuse the system?
- For *which* purposes will the evaluation be conducted—pro forma, confirmation, growth, or employment decisions?

Evaluations should be neither ceremonial congratulations nor reminiscent of Franz Kafka's story "The Trial," in which the protagonist is suddenly arrested and must defend his innocence against a charge about which he can receive no information.

Community college human resource leaders, deans, and chairs are advised to review their processes and procedures for evaluation using *The Personnel Evaluation Standards,* developed by the Joint Committee on Standards for Educational Evaluation (1988). This publication describes four standards:

- *Propriety standards* require that evaluations be conducted legally, ethically, and with due consideration for the welfare of the individuals being evaluated and of clients of the evaluation.
- *Utility standards* guide evaluations so that they will be informative, timely, and influential.
- *Feasibility standards* develop evaluation systems that are as easy to implement as possible, efficient in their use of time and resources, adequately funded, and viable from a number of standpoints.
- *Accuracy standards* require that the obtained information be technically accurate and that the conclusions be linked logically to the data.

In addition, Stuffelbeam and Pullin (1998) propose adding a fifth standard of legal viability indicating that the personnel evaluation system should meet the requirements of all federal, state, and local laws, as well as case law, contracts, collective bargaining agreements, and local board policies and regulations or institutional statutes or bylaws, so that evaluators can successfully conduct fair, efficient, and effective personnel evaluations (p. 17). Although employee evaluation systems should be built with the aforementioned standards central to the construction, the other critical component is the evaluator.

Evaluating someone's performance is not any easy task. To do it right, the evaluator needs knowledge, skill, and a caring attitude. It is important to have knowledge of the evaluation process, the performance standards being evaluated, and the legal parameters that structure the evaluation. Skill in compiling, interpreting, and communicating information is required. Finally, an attitude that defines the value one places on other human beings is essential to the process.

Policies, Practices, and Attitude

The following are some questions that can guide a review of employment practices. This list is meant to be instructive and thought-provoking rather than exhaustive.

- Are our employment practices, policies, and procedures widely known, clear, and easily understood?
- Do we have policies that protect the employees and applicants from discrimination? Do those policies work? How do we know they work?
- Are we purposefully building a diverse workforce that reflects the diversity of our society?
- Is there a pervasive understanding, a deeply held belief, and a concomitant action that clearly signal that individuals are valued in our organization?
- Do we continually train our staff on changes in the law as well as changes in technology?

David Butler, assistant vice president of human resources (HR) at the University of New Hampshire and consultant to community colleges in California, offers two additional questions: Is HR relevant to senior leadership? Is HR strategic to the organization or merely transactional? (personal communication, Apr. 4, 2003).

Effective employment practices that are consistent with legal rights and responsibilities are necessary in sustaining a fair workplace for employees. The critical work of the community college is sustained through its employees. Consequently, they are the college's most valuable resource. Prudent educational leaders provide for preventive maintenance of buildings to ensure long-term worth and use. They should do no less in addressing the long-term needs of their workforce through fair and effective employment practices.

References

Abram, S. "The Americans with Disabilities Act in Higher Education: The Plight of Disabled Faculty." *Journal of Law and Education,* 2003, *32(1),* 1–20.

Cohen, A. M., and Brawer, F. B. *The American Community College.* (4th ed.) San Francisco: Jossey-Bass, 2003.

DeMitchell, T. A. "A Hostile Environment: Sexual Harassment's Evolving Standard." *International Journal of Educational Reform,* 1994, *3(2),* 220–225.

Hendrickson, R. M. *The Colleges, Their Constituencies, and the Courts.* (2nd ed.) Dayton, Ohio: Education Law Association, 1999.

Joint Committee on Standards for Educational Evaluation. *The Personnel Evaluation Standards.* Thousand Oaks, Calif.: Sage, 1988.

Kaplin, W. A., and Lee, B. A. *The Law of Higher Education: A Comprehensive Guide to Legal Implications of Administrative Decision Making.* (3rd ed.) San Francisco: Jossey-Bass, 1995.

Stuffelbeam, D. L., and Pullin, D. "Achieving Legal Viability in Personnel Evaluations." *Journal of Personnel Evaluation in Education,* 1998, *11,* 215–230.
Yudof, M. G., Kirp, D. L., and Levin, B. *Educational Policy and the Law.* (3rd ed.) St. Paul, Minn.: West, 1992.

Legal References

Alexander v. Choate, 469 U.S. 287 (1985).
Brown v. Board of Education of Topeka, 347 U.S. 483 (1954).
Fisher v. Asheville-Buncombe Technical Community College, 857 F. Supp. 465 (W.D.N.C. 1993).
Gratz v. Bollinger, 123 S.Ct. 2411 (2003).
Griggs v. Duke Power Company, 401 U.S. 424 (1971).
Grutter v. Bollinger, 123 S.Ct. 2325 (2003).
Harris v. Forklift Systems, Inc., 114 S.Ct. 367 (1993).
Henson v. Dundee, 682 F.2d 897, 902 (1982).
Horton v. Board of Trustees of Community College District No. 508, 1996 U.S. Dist. LEXIS (N.D. Ill. May 15, 1996) *aff'd* 1997 U.S. Dist. LEXIS 2470 (7th Cir. 1997).
La Fleur v. Wallace State Community College, 955 F.Supp. 1406 (M.D. Ala. 1996).
Lewis v. Chattahoochee Valley Community College, 136 F.Supp. 2d 1232 (M.D. Ala. 2001).
McDonnell Douglas Corporation v. Green, 411 U.S. 792 (1973).
Meritor Savings Bank v. Vinson, 106 S.Ct. 2399 (1986).
Motzkin v. Trustees of Boston University, 938 F.Supp. 983 (D. Mass. 1996).
Nabozny v. Podlesny, 92 F.3d 446 (7th Cir. 1996).
Oncale v. Sundowner Offshore Services, Inc., 523 U.S. 742 (1998).
Purrington v. University of Utah, 996 F.2d 1025 (10th Cir. 1993).
Romer v. Evans, 516 U.S. 620 (1996).
Schroeder v. Hamilton School District, 282 F.3d 946 (7th Cir. 2002).
Southeastern Community College v. Davis, 442 U.S. 397 (1979).
Wygant v. Jackson Board of Education, 106 S.Ct. 1842 (1986).

TODD A. DEMITCHELL *is professor and chair of the Department of Education at the University of New Hampshire.*

This chapter reviews the three-decade history of collective bargaining at community colleges and analyzes how collective bargaining has altered critical areas in the life of community colleges.

Collective Bargaining and Community Colleges

Richard J. Boris

In its thirty-year history, collective bargaining has become a fact of academic life at American colleges and universities. Although the Supreme Court's *Yeshiva* decision (*National Labor Relations Board v. Yeshiva University,* 1980) has largely impeded unionization at private colleges and universities, collective bargaining has set deep roots in both two-year and four-year public institutions (Euben and Hustoles, 2003). "About 45 percent of the 3,331 institutions of higher education are public, and they employ about 71 percent of the roughly 741,000 faculty and enroll about 78 percent of the over 13 million students in higher education. More than half of these public institutions (about 61 percent) are unionized" (Rhoades, 1993, p. 312).

The National Center for the Study of Collective Bargaining in Higher Education and the Professions (hereafter referred to as the National Center), now in its thirty-first year, has monitored collective bargaining developments. Basing their analysis on data provided by the National Center, Euben and Hustoles (2003) concluded that academic professionals are among the United States' most organized workforce: "The National Center for the Study of Collective Bargaining in Higher Education and the Professions found as of 1997 that more than 250,000 faculty were represented in collective bargaining. Over 96% of union-represented faculty members are in the public sector: public colleges and universities employ nearly 240,000 unionized faculty on more than 1,000 campuses, of which about 125,000 are faculty at four-year institutions. There are about 11,000 unionized faculty at about 70 private higher education institutions."

With the overwhelming majority of community colleges being public institutions, that is where academic unionism has made the strongest gains.

Over two-thirds of the collective bargaining units are at two-year colleges, and over 40 percent of the faculty members represented by academic unions teach at community colleges (Annunziato, 1995). To be sure, unionization is not restricted to classroom faculty. Depending on employment category, it is estimated that from a third to nearly a half of nonclassroom personnel are unionized (Hurd, 1995).

Faculty unionization is a complex phenomenon. There are three national union affiliates: the National Education Association, the United Federation of Teachers, and the American Association of University Professors. In addition, there are statewide organizations—New York State United Teachers, for example—with which most local union chapters are affiliated. Some campus-based union locals are affiliated with more than one national organization, and there are community colleges at which faculty members are represented by different bargaining agents on separate campuses (Annunziato, 1995).

Historically, the primary beneficiaries of collective bargaining have been full-time faculty. Contingent or nontraditional faculty, the dominant teaching cohort at community colleges, have recently begun to organize, sometimes in concert with full-time faculty organizations and sometimes independently or with unions such as the United Auto Workers that earlier did not represent academic employees. Although the national unions share many goals, two failed merger initiatives (in 1995 and 1998) by the National Education Association and the American Federation of Teachers point to tense undercurrents within the union movement.

Legal Context for Collective Bargaining Since 1980

When American academic unions first began to organize faculty and staff, the unions targeted colleges and universities in both the public and private sectors. Approximately ninety private institutions were organized during academic unionism's first decade (American Association of University Professors, 2002). In 1980, the *Yeshiva* decision radically altered the collective bargaining landscape. By a 5-to-4 vote, the Supreme Court held that academic professionals at private universities were managerial employees because of their participation in shared governance; thus they were denied the right to bargain collectively and were excluded from protection by the National Labor Relations Board (NLRB). Despite years of political action by all of the national academic unions to overcome this exclusion, private universities and colleges for the most part remain unorganized. On several campuses—Boston University and Fairleigh Dickinson University, for example—faculty unions were decertified following the *Yeshiva* decision (American Association of University Professors, 2002). Unionization at private institutions stopped for two decades.

Recently, however, the National Labor Relations Board has issued several decisions permitting union representation at some private (mostly

Catholic) colleges and universities. The regional director of the NLRB held that faculty at Manhattan College in New York were "not managerial" and had the right to bargain collectively, a decision that the NLRB sustained after the college appealed (Leatherman, 2000a). Even though Manhattan College faculty won the right to organize, ultimately they voted against union representation. Nonetheless, the national academic unions have been cautious about declaring a breakthrough because there have been contradictory rulings in similar academic settings. At the Sage Colleges, for example, the NLRB denied professors the right to collective bargaining despite their claim that academic decision making did not meet the *Yeshiva* test of shared governance and collegiality. In 2001, graduate assistants at New York University won NLRB approval to bargain collectively, and their peers at several major private universities have sought representation.

Most community colleges, because they are public institutions, have been exempt from the *Yeshiva* strictures. The right of community college faculty to bargain collectively has not been disputed. Similarly, community colleges have been exempt from the organizing efforts of graduate students because these institutions do not grant graduate degrees. Collective bargaining in community colleges is subject to the regulations and laws of each state, and state regulation is not uniform. In New York State, for example, public employees, including those at community colleges, do not have the right to strike.

Protecting Terms of Employment

All community colleges derive a substantial portion of their operating revenues from student tuition and fees, but there is no universal funding formula. Beyond tuition and fees, most are supported by a combination of local and state funding plus federal sources. Frequently a one-third (state), one-third (local municipality, county, or taxing district), one-third (tuition) formula is followed (Cohen and Brawer, 2003). The prosperity of the Clinton years was not generally matched by increased resources and budgets for public higher education. The national government and many state and local authorities chose to spend their funds elsewhere or differently, such as on tax cuts or health care. Community colleges, in particular, did not fare well in many states. The current recession-driven shortfall in budgetary assistance is a universal concern: "The recession caused many states to reduce their spending, and funding for public higher education suffered. Aggregate appropriations for higher education in 2002–03 rose by only 1.2 percent. This increase, which was the smallest since 1992–93, was only about one-quarter of the previous year's increase and lower than the rate of inflation. Indeed, thirteen states actually cut their appropriations to higher education. Moreover, in several states in which appropriations rose, the major growth was in direct state aid to students—not in funding for public institutions of higher education" (Ehrenberg, 2003).

Diminishing resources limit what is achievable at the negotiating table, especially for salaries and benefits, and these diminished resources are creating management-labor conflict at both two-year and four-year institutions. Historically, these budgetary realities have limited the percentage of full-time tenure-track faculty to 40 percent of the community college teaching cohort. Significant reliance on nontraditional faculty, both part-timers and non-tenure-track full-timers, is likely to increase.

"Because college enrollments will grow slowly, the number of faculty will show similarly small increases. The ratio of full-timers to part-timers has stabilized at just under 40:60 and will likely remain there as administrators' desires to save money by employing part-timers and faculty organizations' ability to protect full-time positions offset one another" (Cohen, 1999).

Within this complex environment, a negotiated *contract* that defines and protects the terms and conditions of employment is the distinguishing achievement of an organized faculty. Although all academic collective bargaining focuses on the traditional union issues of compensation, such as salary and benefits, and personnel matters, such as retention and promotion, there is no template flexible enough to provide a model contract in the complex world of collective bargaining. This is particularly true for the community colleges, where the settings, funding sources, and internal and external governance structures vary so widely. A review of the National Center's archives leads to the inescapable conclusion that community college contracts differ so greatly as to defy easy classification. However, there are several common denominators in most of these contracts, including the following examples. Faculty covered by collective bargaining agreements often receive automatic cost-of-living adjustments. They have access to formal grievance procedures. Often maximum class enrollments are specified in their contracts, as are committee and nonclassroom responsibilities. Finally, most community college agreements are reopened and renegotiated every two to three years, keeping these and other work-related issues current and viable.

Outcomes of Unionization

Although contracts do vary widely, some general conclusions can be drawn about the economic and noneconomic outcomes of unionization at community colleges. At many community colleges, the faculty's preunionization role in hiring, promotions, and curricular matters resembled more closely that of secondary school teachers than that of university faculty. Although the following statement speaks of the experience at only one college, many union leaders would acknowledge its conclusions:

> Our contracts have been crucial to empowering us. Without a contract, we would have none of the prerogatives that are often taken for granted at four-year colleges and universities. Certainly, we would not be guaranteed a role

in faculty hiring. I arrived at Yuba College before the advent of collective bargaining. I was interviewed for my position by the vice president for academic affairs and the department chair. No department faculty were present. Today, by virtue of collective bargaining, hiring committees consist mostly of faculty members. It is also the contract, and the contract alone, that imposes a collegial evaluation process in a state that mandates by statute post-tenure review for community college faculty [Rubiales, 1998].

Without unionization, community college faculty would be far less likely to enjoy the benefits of academic freedom and tenure, a predictable progression through academic ranks, or due process through grievance mechanisms. Unionization's effects on community college salary and benefit outcomes are also clear. The academic commitments of community college instructors closely parallel those of university peers, and in general their compensation and benefits, especially at lower academic ranks, mirror those of university colleagues (Ehrenberg, 2003). The salary gap at higher ranks is most marked between community college faculty and their counterparts at major research universities. Generally, compensation at community colleges compares favorably with salaries at smaller four-year colleges. However, there are warning signs on the horizon for all institutions of public higher education. Salaries at public institutions are again lagging behind those at private colleges and universities (Ehrenberg, 2003). If all public institutions are competitively disadvantaged in the hiring and retention process, community colleges are the most challenged.

Rarely, however, is contract language restricted to the traditional "trade union" concerns of salary and benefits. Most unions consider themselves zealous guardians of academic culture; therefore, contract language often explicitly enunciates the rules for shared governance and for protection of academic freedom. What the "proper" boundaries were for collective bargaining was a point of conflict when professors first began to organize, and there are still campuses where these boundaries are constantly tested by presidents, administrators, trustees, and faculty representatives. In the early days of collective bargaining, often in academic senates that feared the loss of traditional academic prerogatives through "inappropriate" trade union meddling into academic matters, some faculty members opposed unionization. Today most academic senates and union chapters have negotiated the boundaries of their respective responsibilities, which are in some colleges codified in collective bargaining agreements. Sometimes legislation defines the respective boundaries of academic senates and unions, as is the case in California.

If there is a common thread to be found in the thirty-year history of academic unionism, it is in how members of the organized professoriate are learning to enter the political arena as sophisticated political actors. In part, this political mobilization follows the tradition of mainstream American unionism. But there is more to this thread than just following union traditions. Increasingly, college leaders are professionals trained to administer, publicize, and lobby. Parity at the bargaining table thus requires union political involvement at local, state, and national levels to counterbalance the power of presidents and administrators who have direct access to city halls, state capitals, federal offices, and Congress. In this task, the state and national union organizations provide critical assistance to local union chapters with their research, analysis, and access to officials.

Union and management collaboration to seek public funding, although often praised by both sides, is less common than might be expected. In part, protracted contract negotiations, exacerbated by a depressed economy, have embittered relations on many campuses. Internal conflicts about academic due process and tenure impede public cooperation. In Massachusetts, Florida, California, and New York, the national recession plus state and national politics and ambitions have provoked crises in the university systems by eroding all parties' abilities to resolve these issues locally. Community college faculty and staff unions in California, for example, frequently support candidates in local board of trustees elections (Rubiales, 1998). Despite union and management political savvy, results have been disappointing. Tuition increases and pressures on faculty to improve outcomes and productivity are substituting for increased resources. As David L. Viar, executive director of the Community College League of California, says, "So all the different constituents are left fighting over a piece of the institutional pie. It's my strong belief that greater funding would alleviate a lot of this" (Evelyn, 2002, p. A22).

Looking Ahead

The accomplishments of the first generation of union leaders, who are now passing on their mantles of leadership, were enormous. They built local, state, and national unions that provided for the members of the professoriate at all levels an admirable career path and a predictable career conclusion in dignified retirement.

Union leaders today face harsher internal and external realities.

Earlier assumptions about academic life (tenure, academic freedom, salaries, medical care, and pensions) have altered significantly. Young faculty, many of them in community colleges, face a reality in which hope for tenure is slim, academic freedom is a tough sell, and diminished salaries and benefits are likely to make their academic and personal lives different from those enjoyed by the first generation of unionized faculty. When the time comes, retirement for current young academics might well be unrecognizable compared to what an earlier generation saw as the natural conclusion of a career in academe.

Altered assumptions about academic life are part of a larger tableau. In recent years, not only has public higher education not shared adequately in the prosperity of good times, but it has been harmed when times turned bad. Thirty years ago, when the professoriate was first unionized, there was still a post-*Sputnik* national consensus about the value of higher education. Consequently, the first generation of union leaders, albeit often with conflict and difficulty, was able to leverage generous contracts from the increased resources facilitated by that national consensus.

Now, in addition to diminished consensus and resources, all higher education unions face the challenge of a dramatically altering academic workforce. Contingent and nontraditional faculty are demanding representation that acknowledges their near parity at many baccalaureate institutions and their majority at most community colleges. Fearful about their own academic futures, many young full-time faculty members frequently sympathize with these nontraditional colleagues. The balance of political power in many union locals is becoming uncertain as coalitions form between these two groups. Eugene Anderson (2002) correctly points out that the issue of fairness, of how these instructors are treated, has become significant in higher education.

Many unions responded late not only to the increasing numbers of nontraditional faculty but also to their representation and were slow to comprehend the effects that this growing cohort would have on academe and on the unions themselves. Throughout the United States, nontraditional faculty took matters into their own hands by independently mobilizing on campuses, in statehouses, and elsewhere. Local and national unions now work to engage and organize these academic workers, and competition among unions for nontraditional faculty membership has become fierce (Leatherman, 2000b). The numbers of nontraditional faculty will continue to grow because of predicted massive retirements among faculty hired in the 1970s, because of the nonavailability of full-time replacement positions, and because many university budgets can be balanced only through the hiring of inexpensive academic labor (Jacobson, 2003). In the coming years at the bargaining table, unions will struggle to represent contingent faculty fairly as they demand proportional salaries and decent health and welfare benefits; simultaneously, unions will face perplexing internal issues about their membership rights, political participation, and roles in union leadership.

Few observers have been willing to address publicly how the growing cohort of nontraditional faculty will affect the community college culture. How will curriculum be developed? How will shared governance fare? Who will do committee work? Can part-time community college faculty provide students with the enriched and multidimensional instructional experience that they deserve?

These questions about personnel and resources are not just for union leaders and members. Presidents, administrators, and trustees must also face the effects of changing academic culture on their institutions and the public they serve. Furthermore, several more abstract questions require attention: Why have not colleges and unions *together* better defended their shared world against destabilizing economic and political pressures? Why have not colleges and unions found a common voice that would engage their local communities to better support public higher education? Why have not the *national* organizations found common cause?

Although increased resources would go a long way toward resolving management and labor disputes, an end to the economic recession will not fully alleviate the polarization in some community colleges. Together and separately, administrators and unionists must find the strength to act courageously in the face of strong constituent pressures. Trustees, presidents, and administrators must defend their institutions from unwarranted political pressures and champion their institutional needs in statehouses and governors' offices. Union leaders must negotiate contracts that accord economic security and academic dignity to contingent faculty without sacrificing a dominant full-time professoriate whose survival is critical to academic culture. Administrators, funding sources, and unionists must face productivity issues creatively. Administrators, funding sources, and unionists must agree that a poorly paid, demoralized academic workforce serves no one's interests. Nostalgia for an academic golden age of adequate resources does little to resolve present difficulties. However, collective bargaining negotiations that have sufficient resources to finalize a mutually beneficial contract would be a welcome beginning to a new and constructive normalcy in public higher education.

References

American Association of University Professors. "AAUP Position Paper: Labor Law Reform," June 2002 [http://www.aaup.org/govrel/capthill/2002/02Lablaw.htm]. Accessed Sept. 29, 2003.

Anderson, E. L., *The New Professoriate.* Washington, D.C.: American Council on Education, 2002.

Annunziato, F. "Faculty Collective Bargaining at Exclusively Two-Year Colleges." *National Center for the Study of Collective Bargaining in Higher Education and the Professions Newsletter,* Apr.-May 1995, pp. 1–7.

Cohen, A. M. "The Constancy of Community Colleges," 1999 [http://horizon.unc.edu/projects/seminars/saccr/cohen.asp]. Accessed Sept. 23, 2003.

Cohen, A. M., and Brawer, F. B. *The American Community College.* (4th ed.) San Francisco: Jossey-Bass, 2003.

Ehrenberg, R. G. "Unequal Progress: The Annual Report on the Economic Status of the Profession, American Association of University Professors," 2003 [http://www.aaup.org/surveys/zrep.htm]. Accessed June 5, 2003.

Euben, D., and Hustoles, T. P. "Collective Bargaining: Revised and Revisited, 2001." *AAUP Reports,* rev. Mar. 2003 [http://www.aaup.org/Legal/info%20outlines/legcb.htm]. Accessed June 25, 2003.

Evelyn, J. "A Political Tightrope in California: Community College Leaders Say Faculty Unions' Influence over Trustee Elections Hurts the System." *Chronicle of Higher Education,* Dec. 6, 2002, pp. A22–A23.

Hurd, R. *Directory of Staff Bargaining Agents in Institutions of Higher Education.* New York: National Center for the Study of Collective Bargaining in Higher Education and the Professions, 1995.

Jacobson, J. "Who's Hiring in Mathematics." *Chronicle of Higher Education,* July 24, 2003 [http://chronicle.com/jobs/2003/07/2003072401c.htm]. Accessed Sept. 14, 2003.

Leatherman, C. "The AAUP Reaches Out and Takes Sides." *Chronicle of Higher Education,* June 23, 2000a, p. A-16.

Leatherman, C. "Union Movement at Private Colleges Awakens After a 20-Year Slumber." *Chronicle of Higher Education,* Jan. 21, 2000b, p. A-16.

Rhoades, G. "Retrenchment Clauses in Faculty Union Contracts: Faculty Rights and Administrative Discretion." *Journal of Higher Education,* May-June 1993, pp. 312–347.

Rubiales, D. M. "Collective Bargaining in Community Colleges: A Report from California." *Academe Online,* Nov.-Dec. 1998 [http://www.aaup.org/publications/Academe/98nd/RUB_ND98.HTM]. Accessed June 5, 2003.

Legal Reference

National Labor Relations Board v. Yeshiva University, 444 U.S. 672 (1980).

RICHARD J. BORIS *is professor of political science at York College, City University of New York (CUNY), and executive director of the National Center for the Study of Collective Bargaining in Higher Education and the Professions at Hunter College, CUNY. He has served as chapter chair of the Professional Staff Congress at York College and as vice president and president of the Professional Staff Congress's CUNY-wide organization.*

*This chapter provides an overview of academic freedom
and tenure as applied to the community college.*

Academic Freedom and Tenure

Richard Fossey, R. Craig Wood

Academic freedom and tenure are two concepts that go to the very heart of higher education in the United States. Public or private, secular or religious, most American colleges and universities affirm the principles of academic freedom and tenure. Although a few higher education institutions have experimented with various types of nontenured employment arrangements (Gappa, 1996), the vast majority of postsecondary institutions continue to maintain tenure status for faculty members who meet institutional criteria.

Indeed, the concepts of academic freedom and tenure are closely linked. Academic freedom can be defined as the freedom of faculty members to research, write, teach, and publish without fear of retribution based on the unpopularity of their ideas (American Association of University Professors, [1970] 2002). Tenure is generally defined as the right of a faculty member to continuous employment, which cannot be terminated without adequate cause (generally including financial exigency) or without due process.

Both concepts are designed to enable scholars to pursue their academic work without fear of arbitrary dismissal or retribution. Nevertheless—although both concepts greatly benefit American faculty members—their purpose is not simply to provide job security for professors. Rather, as one court noted with regard to the concept of tenure, the "general welfare" of our society is promoted by the pursuit and free distribution of uninhibited scholarship (*AAUP v. Bloomfield College,* 1974, pp. 853–854).

Over the years, the concepts of academic freedom and tenure have been the subject of litigation, and a body of law has developed that shows how these terms are recognized and understood in higher education. The following discussion summarizes how these two important principles have been articulated by American courts.

Tenure: What Is It?

A commonly accepted understanding of tenure is as follows: "At the expiration of a period of probation, commonly not to exceed six years of full-time service, a faculty member is either to be accorded 'tenure' or to be given a terminal appointment for the ensuing academic year. Thereafter, the professor can be discharged only for 'just cause' or other permissible circumstances and only after a hearing before a body of his or her academic peers" (Finkin, 1996, p. 3).

In the absence of tenure, an instructor's contract is typically a generic document in which the instructor agrees to teach for a certain period of time (normally a semester or an academic year) for an agreed sum of money. Generally, the commencement date and the termination date are stated in the contract. Thus nontenured instructors have no expectation of employment beyond the term of their contracts, although in some instances their contract rights may give them extensive job protection (Gappa, 1996).

Tenure Rights and the Constitution: Due Process

Public institutions are bound by constitutional constraints in their relationships with employees, and the courts have ruled that at least some forms of public employment constitute a constitutionally protected property interest that a public institution may not take away without affording due process. Tenured faculty members at public institutions definitely have property interests in continued employment and cannot be discharged prior to receiving due process. At minimum, due process would include notice of the grounds for termination, a hearing in which the instructor would have the opportunity to rebut the stated charges, and an unbiased tribunal.

Formal policy that ensures due process for tenured faculty facing dismissal may be set forth in state laws, in a state governing board policy, in the policies of individual institutions, or in collective bargaining agreements. Nevertheless, in nearly all cases, grounds for dismissing a tenured faculty member fall within the following broad categories (Smith and Fossey, 1995):

- Incompetence—generally defined as a deficiency in physical, intellectual, or moral ability or the failure or inability to perform the requirements of the job.
- Insubordination—refusal to abide by reasonable rules and regulations or refusal to follow reasonable directives of a superior.
- Immorality—sexual or financial misconduct, use or sale of illegal drugs, or an act that constitutes a serious crime, whether or not the act results in a criminal conviction.
- Neglect of duty—failure to carry out job responsibilities or carelessness in performing job duties. Usually, a tenured faculty member can be dismissed

for neglect of duty only when it is shown that the faculty member's neglect was knowing, intentional, or deliberate.

Published court cases reveal that tenured faculty members are rarely dismissed or even sanctioned for anything less than very serious misconduct such as soliciting sex in a public restroom (*Corstvet v. Boger,* 1985), exploitation of graduate students (*San Filippo v. Bongiovanni,* 1992), or serious sexual harassment (*Levitt v. University of Texas at El Paso,* 1985). There are very few published court cases involving the dismissal of a tenured faculty member for poor-quality scholarship, lack of scholarship, poor teaching, or inadequate performance as a student adviser.

Is it possible for a college or university to have a tenure policy in place even though no formal tenure system had been adopted? In *Perry v. Sindermann* (1972), the U.S. Supreme Court ruled on a case in which a junior college teacher's contract was not renewed and the teacher was given no opportunity for a hearing. The Court said that the institution may have created a de facto tenure system if it had policies and practices in place that gave the teacher a reasonable and objective belief that he enjoyed the benefits of tenure.

In fact, the college's faculty guide contained the following language that Sindermann relied on to support his argument that the college had a de facto tenure policy:

> Teacher Tenure. Odessa College has no tenure system. The Administration of the College wishes the faculty member to feel that he has permanent tenure as long as his teaching services are satisfactory and as long as he displays a cooperative attitude toward his co-workers and his superiors, and as long as he is happy in his work.

If a de facto tenure system existed, the Court concluded, the teacher could not be discharged without being afforded the right to procedural due process.

Although tenure is not constitutionally protected at private institutions, most have tenure structures similar to those that exist in public colleges and universities and that include the right to due process whenever a faculty member's tenure is threatened.

Do nontenured instructors have a right to a due process hearing if their term contracts are nonrenewed? The Supreme Court has said no. In *Board of Regents v. Roth* (1972), the court ruled that procedural due process was not required when a public university elected not to renew a nontenured professor's contract. According to the court, the nontenured professor had no constitutionally protected interest in continued employment; and thus, the Court ruled, the university could simply choose not to rehire the professor when his term contract expired.

Roth's holding does not mean that nontenured instructors are never entitled to a due process hearing when faced with termination. Even nontenured employees are entitled to due process if they are terminated on the basis of allegations that besmirch their reputations or impose a stigma on them. Furthermore, they are entitled to a hearing if they allege that their nonrenewal was based on some unconstitutional motive—retaliation against an instructor for engaging in protected speech, for example, or a termination based on racial prejudice.

Moreover, many public institutions go beyond what the Constitution requires when terminating nontenured instructors, even though they are not obligated to do so. Often state law or university policy provides for at least an informal hearing in which nontenured instructors may request some explanation for their nonrenewal. Obviously, an institution should adhere to applicable state laws and its own policy requirements.

Academic Freedom

At its essence, academic freedom encompasses two notions. First, academic freedom asserts the principle that faculty members in higher education are free to research, write, teach, and publish without fear of retribution based on the unpopularity of their ideas (American Association of University Professors, [1970] 2002). Second, postsecondary institutions have the freedom to conduct the academic enterprise free from unreasonable governmental intrusion. At a minimum, the institution's right to academic freedom includes the right to determine on academic grounds "who may teach, what may be taught, how it shall be taught, and who may be admitted to study" (*Sweezy v. New Hampshire*, 1957, p. 263).

The Supreme Court has identified academic freedom as a concept that is closely associated with the constitutional right to free speech under the First Amendment, holding that a governmental investigation into the subject matter of a university teacher's lectures "was an invasion [of the teacher's] liberties in the areas of academic freedom and political expression," areas in which government should be extremely reticent to intrude" (*Sweezy v. New Hampshire*, 1957, p. 250). Kaplin and Lee (1995) confirm that courts have been reluctant to involve themselves in disputes concerning "course content, teaching methods, grading, or classroom behavior" (p. 305). Furthermore, in *Keyishian v. Board of Regents of the State University of New York* (1967), the Supreme Court said that academic freedom is "a special concern of the First Amendment, which does not tolerate laws that cast a pall of orthodoxy over the classroom" and described the college classroom as a "marketplace of ideas" where the nation's future leaders would be trained through exposure to a robust exchange of opinions, rather than some authoritative prescription of information (p. 603).

Although the Supreme Court has recognized academic freedom as an important principle in higher education, scholars agree that it has not clearly defined the contours of the concept—particularly the academic freedom rights of faculty members (Chang, 2001; DeMitchell, 2002; Zirkel, 1988). Nor has the Supreme Court clarified how the academic freedom rights of colleges and universities should be balanced against the rights of individual scholars. Based on a series of published cases that have been issued by the lower federal courts, the courts examine a scholar's academic freedom claims almost exactly the way they examine free speech claims by nonacademic public employees. In other words, the courts have not carved out a constitutional niche for academic freedom that is separate and apart from the constitutional rights of all public employees to engage in free speech (*Urofsky v. Gilmore,* 2000).

In general, the Supreme Court's analytical framework requires courts to ask two questions. First, does the public employee's disputed speech involve a matter of public concern? In other words, does the speech touch on some social or political issue that is of interest to the public, or is it merely speech that pertains solely to an employment dispute and has little interest to anyone other than the affected employee? If the speech does not touch on a matter of public concern, as the Supreme Court instructed in *Connick v. Myers* (1983), the speech does not implicate the First Amendment and has no constitutional significance. If a court finds that a public employee's challenged speech does in fact involve a matter of public concern, the Supreme Court requires a second question to be asked: Does the constitutional right of the public employee to speak on a particular topic outweigh the public institution's interest as an employer in maintaining the efficiency of the workplace? (*Pickering v. Board of Education,* 1968). In other words, a public employee's right to speak in a public agency workplace must be balanced against the negative impact the speech might have in detracting from the agency's effective operations, including its impact on employee morale, workplace harmony, or the employee's relationship with a superior (Alexander and Alexander, 2001).

When one examines the body of federal case law on claims of academic freedom, it is clear that the courts have not always acted with total consistency. Nevertheless, when taken together, the decisions articulate a commonsense understanding of a faculty member's academic freedom rights, one that is generally consistent with the norms of the mainstream academic community.

Lower Court Rulings on Faculty Academic Freedom

Over the years, the federal courts have addressed a college faculty member's right to academic freedom on many occasions. In general, these cases can be divided into four categories: academic freedom rights outside the classroom, academic freedom rights inside the classroom, the academic freedom right to assign grades and assess students, and academic rights concerning institutional evaluations of a faculty member.

Academic Freedom Rights Outside the Classroom. Most faculty members in American colleges and universities enjoy an academic freedom right to write, publish, and speak in the public arena without the fear of retribution. This right is so well understood that there are few recorded cases in this area. A 1992 opinion out of the Second Circuit Court of Appeals (*Levin v. Harleston,* 1992) illustrates the concept. Michael Levin, a tenured philosophy professor at City University of New York, became the subject of student protests based on his published writings that criticized affirmative action and suggested that the average black person was less intelligent than the average white person. The university responded to student complaints by creating an alternate section of Levin's philosophy class and allowing students who were disaffected with Levin to transfer to the alternate section. None of Levin's students had ever complained of unfair treatment because of race. In addition, the university created an ad hoc committee charged with determining whether Levin's racial views affected his teaching ability.

Levin sued, claiming that the creation of an alternative class section stigmatized him solely because of the ideas he had expressed and that the formation of a special committee to investigate him had a chilling effect on his constitutional right to free speech. Although the university argued that Levin's out-of-classroom expressions harmed students and the educational process within the classroom, the Second Circuit disagreed. In the court's opinion, the creation of a "shadow section" of Levin's class, which encouraged the size of his class to shrink, was a First Amendment violation. The court also said that the commencement of disciplinary proceedings or the threat of commencing them, based solely on Levin's off-campus statements, violated his First Amendment rights.

Note that the *Levin* case was decided on constitutional grounds without reliance on any separately articulated academic freedom right. But the decision makes clear that a faculty member at a public institution enjoys a First Amendment right to speak and write on controversial subjects, a right consistent with the higher education community's generally held definition of academic freedom. On the other hand, as the Seventh Circuit recently stated, a professor's boorish barroom prattle is not constitutionally protected.

In *Trejo v. Shoben* (2003), a state university terminated a nontenured professor's employment after an investigation concluded that the professor had behaved inappropriately at a hotel bar during an academic conference and had engaged in other boorish behavior toward women. The professor sued, alleging a violation of his right to free speech, arguing, among other things, that his barroom discussion about the sexual behavior of nonhuman primates was an "academic and intellectual debate" that was protected by the First Amendment. The Seventh Circuit rejected this argument, saying:

> We hold that Trejo's statements in Toronto regarding the sexual behavior of non-human primates. . . . failed to address an issue of public concern under

Connick and *Pickering.* The statements were simply parts of a calculated type of speech designed to further Trejo's private interests in attempting to solicit female companionship. . . . The record before us makes clear that Trejo was prattling on before a table of acquaintances. . . . drinking alcoholic beverages in a . . . . bar rather than lecturing to students in a classroom setting on a topic relevant to their field of study. . . . The record is barren of any evidence. . . . [that Trejo's] remarks were designed to serve any truly pedagogic purpose [p. 887].

Together, *Levin* and *Trejo* sketch the broad boundaries of a public college or university professor's First Amendment rights concerning off-campus speech. As *Levin* illustrates, a professor's off-campus speech on matters of public concern is constitutionally protected, even if offensive. On the other hand, as *Trejo* shows, a professor's off-color comments, vulgarities, and sexual innuendo do not touch on matters of public concern and are not sheltered under the First Amendment or any reasonable notion of academic freedom.

Academic Freedom Rights Inside the Classroom. A faculty member's academic freedom rights are more circumscribed when the faculty member's speech occurs inside the college classroom. In the classic case of *Martin v. Parrish* (1986), the Fifth Circuit Court of Appeals ruled that an economics instructor could be discharged for barraging his students with profanity. Students complained, and the community college fired him. The instructor sued, claiming that the college violated his right to freedom of speech and his right to academic freedom.

In ruling for the college, the Fifth Circuit relied on a Supreme Court decision that had upheld a school district's right to censor a high school student's lewd and vulgar speech (*Bethel School District No. 403 v. Fraser,* 1986). Admittedly, the Court said, the *Bethel* decision had involved a high school audience, not college students. "Nevertheless," the court continued, "we view the role of higher education as no less pivotal to our national interest" (p. 585). The Fifth Circuit characterized Martin's speech as a superfluous attack on a "captive audience" (p. 586), which had no academic purpose. Such speech, the court concluded, enjoyed no constitutional protection.

Since *Martin v. Parrish,* a number of courts have addressed the constitutional limitations on college instructors' classroom speech. In a 1995 case, for example, the Sixth Circuit Court of Appeals (*Dambrot v. Central Michigan University,* 1995), relying in part on *Martin,* upheld a Michigan university that fired a basketball coach for using an offensive racial slur in the presence of student athletes. The coach argued that he used the word as a motivational tool and claimed an academic freedom privilege, but the Sixth Circuit was not persuaded. In the court's view, the coach's statement did not involve a matter of public concern and hence was not entitled to constitutional protection. Moreover, the court said the university had a right to disapprove of his use of the slur as a motivational strategy. Using the term had nothing to do with "the marketplace of ideas" or the realm of academic freedom.

In *Bishop v. Aronov* (1991), the Eleventh Circuit ruled that a university could prohibit a professor from discussing his religious views in his physiology classes. The court ruled that classroom time was reserved for instruction on the topic of the course, and the university had the prerogative to regulate the professor's classroom speech. Likewise, in *Rubin v. Ikenberry* (1996), a federal district court ruled that a professor's sexual remarks in an education methods class had nothing to do with the subject matter he was teaching, did not address issues of public concern, and so were not protected by the First Amendment or principles of academic freedom.

On the other hand, in *Hardy v. Jefferson Community College* (2001), the Sixth Circuit upheld the right of a part-time instructor to use several inflammatory words because the use of the words in a course on interpersonal relations was appropriate to the topic of the course. A Kentucky community college had declined to renew the instructor's contract after receiving complaints about his use of the words. The college's action, in the Sixth Circuit's view, violated the instructor's constitutional right to free speech.

Finally, the 1994 case of *Silva v. University of New Hampshire* (cited in Fossey and Roberts, 2002) stands outside the mainstream of federal jurisprudence on academic freedom and deserves mention. In that case, a university attempted to sanction a tenured professor who used sexual metaphors to students in a freshman writing class. Eight students submitted written complaints, describing the professor's language as "vulgar," "inappropriate," and "demeaning." The university created another section of the professor's course for students who preferred another instructor, and twenty-six students transferred out of the professor's class. After administrative proceedings, the university sanctioned the professor for engaging in sexual harassment and put him on a one-year leave without pay. Silva sued in federal court, where he won an injunction against the university and reinstatement to his job with full pay and tenure. In its opinion, the court ruled that the professor's remarks related to a matter of public concern. Specifically, the court said his expressions were related to the issue of whether speech that offends a particular group should be permitted in the nation's schools. In addition, the court ruled that the university had breached the academic freedom provision in its collective bargaining agreement with faculty.

In the opinion of several commentators, the *Silva* ruling is unfortunate (Woodward, 1999; DeMitchell and Fossey, 1996; Fossey and Roberts, 2002). Sexual harassment in the classroom "has nothing to do with academic freedom" (Dziech and Weiner, 1990, p. 179). It hinders the learning environment, violates federal sex discrimination law, and can subject a college to civil liability. Fortunately, *Silva* stands virtually alone in protecting offensive language in the classroom. As noted, other courts have supported higher education institutions that have sanctioned instructors for uncivil classroom language.

Right to Assign Grades and Make Curricular Decisions. Faculty members might assume that they have an unfettered right to choose curriculum materials for their courses and to assign grades. Federal case law indicates that this right is far from absolute.

Perhaps the most strongly worded court opinion in this area is a 1998 case, *Edwards v. California University of Pennsylvania* (1998). Edwards, a tenured professor, was disciplined for using an unapproved syllabus in an introductory course on educational media after a student complained that he was using the course to advance religious ideas (p. 489). Edwards sued, claiming a violation of his First Amendment rights.

Edwards lost his case at the trial court level, and the Third Circuit affirmed the trial court's decision. "As a threshold matter," the Third Circuit said, "we conclude that a public university professor does not have a First Amendment right to decide what will be taught in the classroom" (p. 491). The university, the court said, has the right to make content-based decisions when shaping its curriculum; and a professor has no constitutional right to choose course materials that are contrary to the university's orders.

Nor do professors have the final say with regard to students' grades. In *Parate v. Isibor* (1989), a university chose not to renew a professor's appointment because he refused to change a student's grade from a B to an A. The Sixth Circuit ruled that the assignment of a grade is a symbolic communication and that the university had violated the professor's First Amendment rights by seeking to compel him to change a grade. Nevertheless, the court also said that a professor "has no constitutional interest in the grades which his students ultimately receive" (p. 829). Therefore, as a constitutional matter, the university can change a professor's grade even though it could not compel the professor himself to do so.

In 2001, the Third Circuit went even further. In *Brown v. Armenti* (2001), the Third Circuit rejected the Sixth Circuit view that a professor's grade is constitutionally protected expression. "A public university professor does not have a First Amendment right to expression via the school's grade assignment procedures," the Third Circuit ruled. On the contrary, grading is a pedagogic activity, "subsumed under the university's freedom to decide how a course is to be taught" (p. 75).

Parate and *Brown* are in harmony with an earlier case in which James Lovelace, a nontenured teacher, claimed that the university had violated his right to academic freedom when it failed to renew his teaching contract due to his rigorous grading standards (*Lovelace v. Southeastern Massachusetts University*, 1986). According to Lovelace, the university acted in response to student complaints that his course was too hard and his homework assignments were too demanding.

The First Circuit Court of Appeals rejected Lovelace's arguments, saying, "Whether a school sets itself up to attract and serve only the best and brightest students or whether it instead gears its standards to a broader, more average population is a policy decision which, we think, universities must be allowed to set. And matters such as course content, homework load, and grading policy are core university concerns, integral to implementation of this policy decision" (p. 425). In the court's view, Lovelace's claim that his grading policy is constitutionally protected would unduly restrict the university in defining and performing its educational mission. The First Amendment, the court observed, "does not require that each non-tenured professor be made a sovereign unto himself" (p. 426).

Although the Lovelace case involved a nontenured professor, the court's decision did not turn on that point. Thus the court's reasoning would seem to apply to tenured as well as nontenured faculty members.

Taken together, these cases indicate that higher education institutions have the final say on curriculum content, choice of curriculum materials, grading policies, and assignment of student grades. A faculty member's grading decision may be constitutionally protected expressive speech (although the courts disagree on that proposition), but the final decision about what grade should be assigned rests with the institution, not the instructor.

Rights Regarding Teaching Evaluations. In at least two cases, professors sued their institutions on constitutional grounds because they objected to outside evaluation of their instructional methods. In both cases, the universities prevailed.

In *Wirsing v. Board of Regents* (1990), a tenured professor at the University of Colorado refused to administer a standardized faculty evaluation form to her students, based on her position that the evaluation process was contrary to her theory of education. In response, the university withheld her merit pay increase. Wirsing sued, arguing that the university had violated her right to academic freedom. A federal trial court dismissed the professor's suit, saying, "Academic freedom is not a license for activity at variance with job-related procedures and requirements" (p. 553, citing *Stastney v. Board of Trustees,* 1982). Dr. Wirsing may have a constitutionally protected right to disagree with the university's evaluation policy, the court said, but "she has no right to evidence her disagreement by failing to perform the duty imposed upon her as a condition of employment" (p. 553).

Wirsing is in harmony with an older Sixth Circuit opinion in which the court upheld a university's decision not to renew an untenured professor's contract based on institutional concerns about her pedagogical style and teaching methods (*Hetrick v. Martin,* 1973). The professor had argued that her teaching methods were constitutionally protected under the First Amendment, but the Sixth Circuit disagreed. "Whatever may be the ultimate scope of the amorphous 'academic freedom' guaranteed to our Nation's teachers and students, . . . it does not encompass the right of a non-tenured teacher to have her teaching style insulated from review by her superiors when they determine whether she has merited tenured status just because her methods and philosophy are considered acceptable somewhere within the teaching profession" (p. 709).

Wirsing and *Hetrick* emphasize that college and university faculty members have no constitutional right to avoid institutional evaluation of their teaching performance. However, in both cases, the courts concluded that the evaluation processes were objective and not a subterfuge to punish an instructor for expressing unpopular ideas in the classroom. As the Supreme Court has said in the *Keyishian* case, the college classroom is a "marketplace of ideas." A court might well intervene if it were convinced that an institution that had sanctioned an instructor for unsatisfactory performance had done so for the real purpose of casting "a pall of orthodoxy" over the classroom.

Conclusion

As we have seen, tenure and academic freedom are closely connected, and both concepts serve the function of preserving the right of higher education scholars to teach, research, and publish without fear of retribution. Moreover, both concepts have strong links to the U.S. Constitution. A faculty member's right to academic freedom is akin to a public employee's right to free speech under the First Amendment, and tenure—at least in the public sector—is a property right, which under the Fourteenth Amendment cannot be taken away without affording due process.

In the private sector, of course, institutions do not operate under constitutional constraints with regard to their relationships with faculty members. Professors at private colleges have no First Amendment protection from institutional censor based on their speech, and they enjoy no constitutional right to demand due process in disciplinary or termination proceedings. Nevertheless, reputable private institutions honor the concepts of academic freedom and due process in their policies, procedures, and contracts. As a practical matter, colleges and universities view academic freedom and tenure very much alike, whether they are public or private.

A review of published case law reveals that neither concept is in danger of erosion in American higher education. Very few cases have involved efforts by institutions to sanction a faculty member based on the offensiveness of the faculty member's ideas. Instead, most of the published legal disputes between faculty members and institutions have involved more mundane issues—classroom deportment, sexual harassment, and various allegations of professional misconduct. On the broad issue of a scholar's right to speak out on important social and political questions or to propound controversial positions on scholarly topics, instructors, courts, and institutions are in broad agreement—academic freedom and tenure are alive and well in the nation's colleges and universities.

References

Alexander, K., and Alexander, M. D. (2001). *American Public School Law.* (5th ed) Belmont, Calif.: Wadsworth, 2001.

American Association of University Professors. "1940 Statement of Principles on Academic Freedom and Tenure with 1970 Interpretive Comments." (rev. ed.) Washington, D.C.: American Association of University Professors, 2002 (originally published 1970). [http://www.aaup.org/statements/Redbook/1940stat.htm]. Accessed Jan. 17, 2004.

Chang, A. W. "Note: Resuscitating the Constitutional 'Theory' of Academic Freedom." *Stanford Law Review*, 2001, *55*, 915–966.

DeMitchell, T. A. "Academic Freedom—Whose Rights: The Professor's or the University's?" *Education Law Reporter*, 2002, *168*, 1–19.

DeMitchell, T. A., and Fossey, R. "At the Margin of Academic Freedom and Sexual Harassment: *Silva v. University of New Hampshire." Education Law Reporter*, 1996, *111*, 13–32.

Dziech, B. W., and Weiner, L. *The Lecherous Professor: Sexual Harassment on Campus.* (2nd ed.) Urbana: University of Illinois Press, 1990.

Finkin, M. W. *The Case for Tenure.* Ithaca, N.Y.: ILR Press, 1996.

Fossey, R., and Roberts, N. "Academic Freedom and Uncivil Speech: When May a College Regulate What an Instructor Says in the Classroom?" *Education Law Reporter,* 2002, *168*(2), 549–564.

Gappa, J. M. *Off the Tenure Track: Six Models for Full-Time Nontenurable Appointments.* Washington, D.C.: American Association for Higher Education, 1996.

Kaplin, W. A., and Lee, B. A. *The Law of Higher Education: A Comprehensive Guide to Legal Implications of Administrative Decision Making.* (3rd ed.) San Francisco: Jossey-Bass, 1995.

Smith, M. C., and Fossey, R. *Crime on Campus: Legal Issues and Campus Administration.* Phoenix, Ariz.: Oryx Press and American Council on Education, 1995.

Woodward, L. M. "Collision in the Classroom: Is Academic Freedom a License for Sexual Harassment?" *Capital University Law Review*, 1999, *27*, 667.

Zirkel, P. A. "Academic Freedom of Individual Faculty Members." *Education Law Reporter*, 1988, *47*, 809–824.

Legal References

AAUP v. Bloomfield College, 322 A.2d 846 (N.J. Super. 1974).

Bethel School District No. 403 v. Fraser, 474 U.S. 814 (1986).

Bishop v. Aronov, 926 F.2d 1066 (11th Cir. 1991).

Board of Regents v. Roth, 408 U.S. 564 (1972).

Brown v. Armenti, 247 F.3d 69 (3rd Cir. 2001).

Connick v. Myers, 461 U.S. 138 (1983).

Corstvet v. Boger, 757 F.2d 223 (1985).

Dambrot v. Central Michigan University, 55 F.3d 1177 (6th Cir. 1995).

Edwards v. California University of Pennsylvania, 156 F.3d 488 (3rd Cir. 1998).

Hardy v. Jefferson Community College, 360 F.3d 671 (6th Cir. 2001), *cert. denied sub. nom. Besser v. Hardy*, 122 S.Ct. (2002).

Hetrick v. Martin, 480 F.2d 705 (6th Cir. 1973).

Keyishian v. Board of Regents of the State University of New York, 385 U.S. 589 (1967).

Levin v. Harleston, 966 F.2d 85 (2nd Cir. 1992).

Levitt v. University of Texas at El Paso, 759 F.2d 1224 (5th Cir.) *cert. denied sub nom. Levitt v. Monroe*, 474 U.S. 1034 (1985).

Lovelace v. Southeastern Massachusetts University, 793 F.2d 419 (1st Cir. 1986).

Martin v. Parrish, 805 F.2d 583 (5th Cir. 1986).
Parate v. Isibor, 868 F.2d 821 (6th Cir. 1989).
Perry v. Sindermann, 408 U.S. 593 (1972).
Pickering v. Board of Education, 391 U.S. 563 (1968).
Rubin v. Ikenberry, 933 F.Supp. 1425 (C.D. Ill. 1996).
San Filippo v. Bongiovanni, 961 F.2d 1125 (3rd Cir.), *cert. denied*, 113 S.Ct. 305 (1992).
Silva v. University of New Hampshire, 888 F.Supp. 293 (D.N.H. 1994).
Stastney v. Board of Trustees, 647 P.2d 496 (Wash. App. 1982), *cert. denied*, 460 U.S. 1071 (1983).
Sweezy v. New Hampshire, 354 U.S. 234 (1957).
Trejo v. Shoben, 319 F.3d 878 (7th Cir. 2003).
Urofsky v. Gilmore, 216 F.3d 401 (4th Cir. 2000).
Wirsing v. Board of Regents, 739 F.Supp. 551 (D.Colo. 1990).

RICHARD FOSSEY, J.D., is Fondren Research Fellow at the Center for Reform of School Systems in Houston, Texas, and a professor in the College of Education at the University of Houston.

R. CRAIG WOOD is the B. O. Smith Research Professor in the College of Education, University of Florida, Gainesville.

This chapter provides an overview of copyright and intellectual property law as it relates to education in general and telecommunicated instruction in particular.

Copyright Issues and Technology-Mediated Instruction

Kenneth D. Salomon, Michael B. Goldstein

Intellectual property has always been at the core of education at all levels, regardless of whether instruction is delivered in a physical classroom or electronically. At the most fundamental level, a professor's lecture notes are his or her intellectual property, and of course the authoring of textbooks is the lifeblood of education. The intellectual property implications of technology-mediated instruction are at once a natural extension of customary rules and an entirely new legal and academic environment.

The widespread use of technology-mediated instruction has raised faculty and administration awareness of copyright issues, including who owns what, what materials can be used in electronic courses, and who is liable when the rules are broken. In 2002, Congress created a new set of copyright rules in the Technology, Education and Copyright Harmonization (TEACH) Act to govern the delivery of courses over interactive digital networks. This chapter provides a brief overview of copyright basics under the 1976 Copyright Act, provides guidance on the implications and application of the TEACH Act, and addresses issues related to ownership of e-courses.

Copyright Protection

Boiled down to its essence, copyright protects the right of authors to be rewarded for their works and the right of the public to have access to them. An author's original expression of ideas and facts that is fixed in a tangible medium such as film, paper, canvas, or software is subject to copyright protection, as are literary, dramatic, musical, artistic, and certain other intellectual works, whether the work is published or unpublished. Facts, ideas, and concepts themselves are not copyrightable because they exist independent of the author. Nor are procedures, processes, principles, discoveries, or methods of operation entitled to copyright protection (Section 102(b) of the 1976 Copyright Act). On the other hand, factual compilations may be copyrighted if there is originality in the selection, coordination, or arrangement of the data. It is the unique way in which an author manipulates, coordinates, and arranges facts and ideas to create "original works of authorship" that are copyrightable. Originality is an absolute essential requirement for copyrightable expression; however, only a modest degree of originality, not novelty, is required.

Automatic Protection. Copyright protection is automatic. Since adoption of the 1976 Copyright Act, copyright protection arises automatically and simultaneously with the act of fixing the original work of authorship in any tangible medium of expression through which the author's work can be perceived or communicated. Since March 1, 1989, a copyright notice is not required to appear on the work to ensure copyright protection. Nevertheless, placing a notice on the work is often beneficial, and doing so remains relevant to the copyright status of older works. A notice informs the public that a work is protected by copyright and identifies the copyright owner and the year of first publication.

Neither filing a copy of the work with the U.S. Copyright Office nor placing a copyright notice on the work is required to obtain copyright protection, although doing both provides the copyright owner with several important benefits, including the ability to elect statutory damages and recovery of attorney's fees for infringements of the owner's exclusive rights (Section 412). The Copyright Office provides instructions and forms for registering different types of works on it.[1]

Exclusive Rights of Copyright Owners. The owner of a copyright obtains what has been called a "bundle of exclusive rights." The bundle of exclusive rights of a copyright owner consists of the rights to reproduce the work; prepare derivatives or adaptations based on the original work; distribute copies of the work to the public by sale or gift or by rental, lease, or lending; perform the work publicly; and display the work publicly (Section 106). The copyright owner may dispose of any or all of his or her exclusive rights in an infinite variety of ways. The transfer rights of copyright owners are spelled out in Sections 201–205 of the 1976 Copyright Act.

Types of Copyright Ownership. Four forms of copyright ownership are recognized by the 1976 Copyright Act: author, joint works, collective works, and works made for hire.

Author. The default position is that the author or creator of the work holds all of the exclusive rights of copyright. In general, the term of copyright protection for works created after 1978 is the lifetime of the author plus seventy years.

Joint. Two or more authors who intend at the time of creation that their individual contributions will be incorporated into inseparable or interdependent parts of a single copyrightable work are considered co-owners under Section 201(a) of the 1976 Copyright Act. This means that while each author owns the entire work and may exploit it independently of the other, each author must make an economic accounting to the other.

Collective Works. Separate and independent contributions that are assembled into a collective whole, such as an encyclopedia or an anthology of short stories, are examples of collective works. The copyright in each separate and independent contribution to the collection is distinct from the copyright in the collection itself. Thus the owner of the copyright of the collective work acquires only the rights to copy and distribute the individual contributions to the collective work as a part of the collective work itself; each contributor retains the copyright to his or her individual work (Section 201(c)).

Works Made for Hire. There are two categories of works made for hire. The first is a work prepared by an employee within the scope of employment. Typically, the employer or other person for whom the work was prepared is the copyright owner unless there is a signed written agreement to the contrary. The second form of work for hire is one specifically ordered or commissioned for use—for example, as a contribution to a collective work, as part of a motion picture or other audiovisual work, or as a secondary part of a work by another author—provided that the parties agree in writing that the work is a work made for hire (Section 101).

Detailed discussion of the types of work covered under each of these categories is beyond the scope of this chapter, as is the determination of whether an individual is an employee or an independent contractor under the work-made-for-hire provision (*Community for Creative Non-Violence v. Reid,* 1989).

Infringement

An infringement is the exercise of any of exclusive rights of a copyright owner (reproduction, adaptation, performance, distribution, and display) without either the permission of the copyright owner (say, through a license) or the authority of one of limitations on those rights established by the 1976 Copyright Act. Infringement is a "strict liability offense," and anyone who helps or enables another person to infringe a copyright may be liable (*Sony Corp. v. Universal Studios,* 1984; *Sega Enterprises Ltd. v. Maphia,* 1996).

A number of easy-to-understand but largely inaccurate myths exist about the ability to use copyrighted works without permission or fear of a claim of infringement, including "(1) a work is not covered by copyright if it lacks a copyright notice; (2) use of small parts of a work is not necessarily an infringement; (3) you can copy a work if you provide attribution to the author; and (4) the addition of something creative to the copyrighted work makes it is a new work and not an infringement." With the possible exception of the fair use defense suggested by myth 2 (depending on the facts of the case), these guidelines are inaccurate and should not be used to guide practice (Brinson and Radcliffe, 1996).

Penalties for Infringement. The 1976 Copyright Act gives federal courts a wide variety of penalties and remedies to impose upon a finding that the defendant committed an infringement, including the following:

- The award of *actual* proven economic *damages* and lost profits
- The award of *statutory damages* of between $750 and $30,000 for the infringement of registered work and up to $150,000 in the case of a willful infringement in lieu of actual damages at the election by the copyright owner before a final judgment in the case of a work that has been registered with the Copyright Office
- The award of *attorney's fees* and costs in the case of a registered work
- The issuance of an *injunction*
- The issuance of an order that the infringing goods be *impounded and destroyed*
- Imposition of *criminal penalties* in the case of willful infringement for commercial advantage or private financial gain, and the *destruction* of infringing copies and the facilities used to manufacture the infringing copies

The availability of each of these remedies in large part hinges on whether or not a work has been registered with the Copyright Office. Owners of unregistered works are typically only eligible to receive compensation for actual economic damages, whereas registered owners may access other remedies (McMillen, 2001; Sections 502–506 of the 1976 Copyright Act).

Infringement by Nonprofit Institutions. Section 504(c)(2) of the 1976 Copyright Act generally permits a court to reduce statutory damages to as little as $200 if it finds that the infringer was unaware and had no reason to believe that use of a copyrighted work constituted an infringement. However, Section 504(c)(2) specifically gives the court authority to remit damages against a nonprofit educational institution, library, or archive if the infringement stems from the actions of an employee acting within the scope of employment who incorrectly believed that the use of a copyrighted work without permission was permitted as a fair use.

Infringement by State Educational Institutions. There are conflicting legal opinions as to whether or not states and state entities can be sued for copyright infringement. Thus far, no final action on corrective legislation has been taken by Congress.

Limitations to Exclusive Rights

Three limitations to exclusive copyrights are particularly relevant to telecommunicated instruction: fair use (Section 107), the educational use exemption (Section 110), and nonprofit libraries and archives (Section 108).

Fair Use. Fair use permits the use of a copyrighted work without the permission of the copyright owner for such purposes as "criticism, comment, news reporting, teaching (including multiple copies for classroom use), scholarship, or research" (Section 107). At the heart of fair use is an assumption of good faith and fair dealing (*Time, Inc., v. Bernard Geis Associates*, 1968). It is crucial to recognize that fair use is not convenient. It does *not* incorporate a simple quantitative limitation or other simple test to ensure that a particular use is fair rather than an infringement (Harper, 2002). To the contrary, in each case, the court must assess four factors laid out by Congress in Section 107:

1. The purpose and character of the use, including whether such use is of a commercial nature or is for nonprofit educational purpose.
2. The nature of the copyrighted work—the courts accord greater protection to creative works than to factual works.
3. The amount and substantiality of the portion used in relation to the copyrighted work as a whole.
4. The effect of the use on the potential market for or value of the copyrighted work.

One area where the fair use test has been specifically applied to an educational setting is the production of course packs or course readers by commercial copy shops. In applying the Section 107 test to the facts, courts have tended to give greater weight to factors 3 and 4 (*Basic Books, Inc., v. Kinko's Graphics Corp.*, 1991; *Princeton University Press v. Michigan Documents Services, Inc.*, 1996).[2]

The Educational Use Exemption. The 1976 Copyright Act includes a specific exemption that permits instructors and students at nonprofit educational institutions to perform or display copyrighted works in a classroom or similar place devoted to instruction in the course of face-to-face teaching activities. If an audiovisual work such as a movie is presented, the copy used must be a lawfully made or acquired copy. Note that Section 110(1) applies only to performance and display rights and does not permit reproduction, distribution, or the making of derivative works. Nevertheless, it is a broad provision.

The TEACH Act

The TEACH Act amended Section 110(2) of the Copyright Act to allow instructors at *accredited nonprofit* educational institutions to use without permission most copyrighted works in e-courses and classes transmitted via interactive digital networks. Specifically, instructors may *perform* via a digital network transmission entire nondramatic literary and musical works and reasonable and limited portions of all other works, including those incorporated in any type of audiovisual work, such as a videotape, CD-ROM, DVD, and film. Furthermore, instructors may *display* via a digital network transmission other types of works, including still images, in amounts comparable to a display of the works in a typical face-to-face live classroom session. The expanded ability to use a broader range of copyrighted works in digital transmissions is bounded by the following important limitations and requirements.

Type of Work. The TEACH Act does *not* apply to works primarily produced for or marketed for the digital distance education market, typically purchased by higher education students individually, and works typically loaned to K–12 students individually, such as textbooks and course packs, or to works that are not lawfully made or acquired.

Content and Access. Works must be directly related and of material assistance to the teaching content and made solely for, and to the extent technologically feasible, limited to reception by students officially enrolled in the class for which the transmission is made. Significantly, unlike the old law, students are not bound to a physical classroom or "similar place devoted to instruction." They may be anywhere—in a classroom, in a dorm room, at work, at home, or in a library.

Systematic Mediated Instructional Activities. The use of the copyrighted work in the transmission must be analogous to a live classroom performance or display and an integral part of the class experience controlled by or under the direct supervision of the instructor.

Technology Protection Measures. The transmitting institution must employ technology protection measures (TPMs) that reasonably prevent the receiving students from retaining the transmission beyond the class session and from redistributing it to others. As new and affordable TPMs come online, the institution needs to upgrade.

Limits on Making Copies. Section 110(2) amendments and the new Section 112(f) added by the TEACH Act allows the transmitting institution to make copies of digital works and to digitize to *portions* of analog works. Once again, however, there are counterbalancing limitations. The copies may be retained only by the transmitting institution and may be used exclusively for making the authorized transmission. Further, the right to make digital copies arises only if (1) there is no digital version of the analog work or (2) there is a digital version but it incorporates TPMs that prohibit its use as authorized by Section 110(2).[3]

Ownership of E-Courseware

Faculty tend to regard e-courseware the same way they view their lecture notes, textbooks, and articles: "This is the product of my own intellectual endeavors, and as the author of the work, I am the owner of it, not my employer." This view is founded on notions of academic freedom and the widely honored tradition on campus that instructors own their academic work product, even if it is created as a job requirement within the scope of employment. On the other hand, administrators are frequently of the view that e-courseware is different from lecture notes and the like and that the institution should be deemed the owner under the work-made-for-hire doctrine, particularly when substantial institutional technology and nonacademic personnel resources may have been used by the instructor to create the e-work or it has been specifically commissioned by the institution.

If an institution elects the work-made-for-hire model for electronic courseware, a key issue may become defining when the use of resources is "substantial." Providing an office with a telephone, Internet connection, and word processor would likely *not* be considered substantial, but a grant of release time, reduced load, a stipend, or the use of specialized equipment or technologies and other employees (course designers, programmers, graphic artists, technicians and other professionals, paid research assistants, studios, media laboratories, CD-ROM facilities, and so on) might be. Another approach to defining *substantial* is the use of resources that fall outside the scope of the faculty member's normal job responsibilities or the use of resources that are not ordinarily available to most faculty members of comparable status.

The debate over ownership is often fueled by an assumption that the e-courseware will be the equivalent of a *New York Times* best-seller. The reality, however, is that the vast majority of e-courseware will not come close to that hallmark, and as a consequence, a fight between faculty and administration over ownership of the e-work may not be worth the effort. Remember that the exclusive rights of a copyright owner can be transferred and assigned. That being the case, is naked ownership of the copyright all that important? It is possible to create a win-win situation if the parties identify what they need and want and then unbundle the rights of ownership to reach those goals.

Formulating an E-Course Ownership Policy. Typically, the faculty member is interested in such issues as attribution; the ability to use the e-work on campus and at a new institution if he or she moves; the ability to update, freshen, and correct content; the right to adapt the original work; revenue sharing; and perhaps the right of first refusal to teach the e-course. The administration is typically interested in such issues as continuity; the ability to assign an instructor to use the e-work for at least a limited period if the creating instructor departs or is unavailable; recovery of investment; revenue sharing; protection of the institution's reputation, particularly with regard to the quality of the e-work; protection of the institution's name and logo; and compliance with conflict-of-interest and commitment policies. With these considerations in mind, one approach to formulating an e-courseware ownership policy would be dividing the works into four categories, as follows:

Individual work—conceived of and created by the faculty member on his or her own time and initiative, individual work does not require substantial institutional resources or supervision. Ownership would reside in the faculty member.

Commissioned work—the institution specifically assigns the faculty member to create the work with or without the use of substantial institutional resources. The commissioned work is generally under the supervision and direction of another institution official. Ownership would reside in the institution.

Institutional work—prepared through the use of substantial institutional resources, however that term is defined on the particular campus, institutional work may progress with or without supervision and direction. Ownership would reside in the institution.

Sponsored work—for works produced under an external grant or contract, ownership will be defined by the funding instrument.

While the employing institution is deemed the owner of institutional and commissioned e-courseware, the creating faculty member could be granted many of the rights of ownership through a royalty-free nonexclusive license. Depending on the terms of the agreement, faculty could make adaptations, corrections, and updates; share in external revenues on a specified formula if the institution markets the e-courseware; teach the e-course on campus; and use it off-campus while an employee and at a new employer institution, subject to compliance with the first institution's policies on conflict of interest and commitment and controlling the use of its name and logo.

Notwithstanding the work-made-for-hire doctrine, it may nevertheless be the policy on a campus to cede ownership of these types of works to the faculty members who created them. In such cases, it could be a condition of ceding ownership that the faculty member give the institution a royalty-free nonexclusive license granting the institution such rights as sharing in external revenues on a specified formula if the faculty member markets the e-courseware externally and controlling the use of the institution's name and logo on the e-courseware, particularly in the case of external sales. Similarly, faculty might grant the institution the right to use the e-work at least for a specified period of time to ensure educational continuity in the event that the faculty member leaves the institution or is unavailable to teach the course and to adapt, correct, and update the e-work, particularly if the faculty member leaves the institution or is unavailable to perform the update.

Resolving e-courseware ownership questions can be done on a case-by-case basis or through collective bargaining or an institutional policy. The following checklist may be useful to faculty and administration in reviewing existing ownership policies and contract provisions or in drafting initial e-courseware ownership positions:

• Inspiration for development of the e-courseware. Does the institution have the right to control the "manner and means" of creation? Does it provide the necessary facilities and resources and the location of the work?

- The impact of state law, if any, on employees of public educational institutions.
- A policy on faculty use of the institution's logo on their works. Use of the logo may increase both the perceived value of the work and the institution's exposure to liability for copyright infringement by faculty members.
- Impact of sponsored research and developmental grants on ownership.
- Definition of "substantial resources." Resources in amount and kind over and above those usually and customarily provided to faculty and the provision of institutional funds, personnel, and facilities such as grant dollars, release time, hardware, software, and use of professional staff and other employees to work on the project may be substantial.
- Ownership of the e-course. Who has responsibility for getting clearances and permissions, bearing the risk of liability, and assuming the duty to protect the copyright? Faculty members must identify all nonoriginal material used in the course and must secure reuse permissions.
- Policy administration. Will the policy dispose of ownership, use, and revenue issues or state the norms for negotiation of written contracts on the basis of the policy?

An Intellectual Property Audit. Whether an institution is about to launch an extensive e-learning program or is already in the midst of one, conducting an institutional intellectual property audit would be prudent. The audit should include updating of existing copyright and ownership policies, ascertaining adequacy of existing licenses and agreements covering copyrighted works, resolving conflict-of-interest and commitment issues, reviewing policies on the use of the institution's name and logo, and checking whether the technological resources of the institution satisfy the requirements of the TEACH Act and other pertinent laws. Questions of ownership and rights to exploit e-works should be resolved in written rather than oral agreements or policies that delineate the ownership and use of the works. Institutional trademarks and service marks that may be used in association with the e-works should be protected, with the most important ones registered with the U.S. and foreign-government trademark offices as appropriate. E-works that are created and used by the institution should be registered with the U.S. Copyright Office.

Conclusion

The purpose of copyright protection is to create a balanced environment that encourages the creation of socially useful works by affording authors reasonable protection from the uncompensated appropriation of their works and affords the public reasonable access to those works. The law has always lagged behind technology, and copyright law is perhaps the poster child of that rule. As technology-mediated learning advances and as modes of distribution improve beyond our wildest imaginings, there will continue to be a need to adapt both the underlying law and institutional policies to maintain the essential balance between fairly protecting the rights and interests of authors and ensuring easy access to this most important medium for the dissemination of knowledge.

Notes

1. See the U.S. Copyright Office Web site [http://lcweb.loc.gov/copyright/reg.html].
2. For further information, see "Coursepacks and Fair Use: Issues Raised by the Michigan Document Services Case" [http://www.utsystem.edu/ogc/intellectual property/michigan.htm]; "Fair Use of Copyrighted Material" [http://www.utsystem. edu/ogc/intellectualproperty/copypol2.htm]; and "Guidelines for Classroom Copying of Books and Periodicals" [http://www.utsystem.edu/ogc/intellectualproperty/ clasguid.htm].
3. For more information about the TEACH Act, see "Distance Education and the TEACH Act" [http://www.ala.org/washoff/teach.html].

References

Brinson, J. D., and Radcliffe, M. F. "An Intellectual Property Law Primer for Multimedia and Web Developers." 1996. [http://www.eff.org/pub/CAF/law/ip-primer]. Accessed Oct. 17, 2003.
Harper, G. "Fair Use of Copyrighted Materials," 2002. [http://www.utsystem.edu/ogc/ intellectualproperty/copypol2.htm]. Accessed Jan. 18, 2004.
McMillen, J. D. *Copyright Ownership in Higher Education: University, Faculty, and Student Rights.* Asheville, N.C.: College Administration Publications, 2001.

Legal References

Basic Books, Inc., v. Kinko's Graphics Corp., 758 F. Supp. 1522 (S.D.N.Y. 1991).
Community for Creative Non-Violence v. Reid, 490 U.S. 730 (1989).
Princeton University Press v. Michigan Documents Services, Inc., 99 F.3d 1381 (6th Cir. 1996), *cert. denied,* 520 U.S. 1156 (1997).
Sega Enterprises Ltd. v. Maphia, 948 F.Supp. 923, 932 (N.D.Cal. 1996).
Sony Corp. v. Universal Studios, 464 U.S. 417, 435 (1984).
Time, Inc., v. Bernard Geis Associates, 293 F.Supp. 130, 146 (S.D.N.Y. 1968).

KENNETH D. SALOMON *is a member of the Washington, D.C., law firm of Dow, Lohnes & Albertson PLLC, where he specializes in government relations and issues involving intellectual property and distributed learning. He was one of the principal negotiators for the higher education community in developing the statutory language adopted by Congress in the TEACH Act of 2002.*

MICHAEL B. GOLDSTEIN *leads the higher education practice of Dow, Lohnes & Albertson, serves as general counsel to the American Association of Community Colleges, and sits on the board of directors of the American Association for Higher Education.*

In our increasingly legalistic environment, the work of the governing board has become much more complex and challenging. Board members today need better training and support to meet these challenges.

Current Governing Board Legal Issues

Timothy K. Garfield

The community college governing board has the ultimate legal authority for the management of the college. Recent trends toward student activism, "shared governance," increasingly complex regulations at both the state and federal levels, and greater scrutiny at the local level have made board responsibilities more difficult. This chapter will address some of the most significant legal issues that community college governing boards currently face. Because the regulations applicable to governing boards are a matter of state (not federal) law and vary widely from state to state, the guidelines provided in this chapter will necessarily be general ones.

The increased complexity of the community college environment underscores the need for boards to establish policy and oversee administrators who implement policy rather than micromanage college operations. Governing board members normally do not devote full time to their board responsibilities. Therefore, they are unlikely to stay current with the myriad laws, regulations, administrative decisions, and cases that affect management decision making; nor are they usually able to gather the detailed factual information that is required for sound executive decisions. Consequently, a governing board's most critical action is the selection of a top administrator who will make or oversee the operational decisions of the college.

Whatever the exact scope of the role that a given governing board plays in the operation of a college, it is clear that the legal authority to act is granted to the board as an entity; individual board members have no authority to act independently to bind or otherwise obligate the college district in any way. This is true even of board officers.

NEW DIRECTIONS FOR COMMUNITY COLLEGES, no. 125, Spring 2004 © Wiley Periodicals, Inc.

Rights of Individual Board Members

Individual board members do have certain rights to information, based on the commonsense principle that specific information is necessary in order to cast an informed and wise vote on issues brought before the board or in order to determine what issues the board should consider. Generally, board members should be allowed access to public and nonpublic records that are necessary for the proper discharge of their duties (*Gabrilson v. Flynn*, 1996). Individual board members typically have the right to review all of the college's or district's financial records, since the fiscal solvency of the institution is a board responsibility. Issues may arise, however, if individual board members request personnel or student records.

State and federal student privacy laws limit student record access to college officials who have a "legitimate educational interest" in obtaining the information contained in the records. Personal conflicts with students and employees are not a sufficient basis on which to obtain access to such records. A similar standard would likely be applied to personnel records, meaning that an individual board member would not have the right to peruse employee personnel records at random. However, if the board member articulates a specific issue relating to the employee's performance and information in the personnel file would be pertinent, the individual board member may have a right to access that information.

In a recent Missouri case, the board president attempted to withhold from the other board members correspondence between the president and the board's attorney concerning alleged misconduct by two board members. The court held that all members of the board, including the members who were the subject of the investigation, had a right to access the letters, which were prepared or solicited by the board president in his official capacity (*State ex rel. Moore v. Brewster*, 2003). Occasionally, a board member's constant requests for information from management will tie up administrative resources to such an extent that the remaining board members should take official action to place reasonable limits on member requests to generate information.

The right of an individual board member to attend an internal meeting between district employees or meetings of district employees with students or parents has been questioned. Generally speaking, there appears to be no legal basis whereby an individual board member could insist on being present at such an internal meeting. Of course, the board as a whole, by a proper vote, could authorize an individual member to attend such meetings unless a student's or employee's privacy rights would be violated by the board member's presence.

Internal Board Relations

One fact does not seem to vary from state to state or district to district: disputes among board members are a daily fact of life. Experienced observers recognize that smooth internal board relations facilitate sound administration of college business. Less time is wasted preparing information for board factions to use in advancing their position, and managers can focus on important issues rather than trying to persuade board members to work collegially. Although the dynamics of intraboard relationships depend to a large degree on the personalities of the board's members, it may be useful for a board to adopt a code of ethics that, while not legally enforceable, board members are expected to follow. Such a code serves as a written reminder that board members serve to advance the interests of the college and not their personal agendas or agendas of a single constituency, such as faculty or taxpayers. The existence of such a code was a significant factor in a Wyoming board's censure of one of its members for attempting to undermine a final majority board decision. The board member, after voting with the majority to submit a property tax assessment to the voters, placed an advertisement in the local newspaper the day before the election encouraging the public to vote against the measure. The board's code of ethics provided that members will "abide by and uphold the final majority decision of the board." The board voted to censure the member, who then sued the board for tarnishing her public reputation in violation of her free speech rights. The court held that the censure, while possibly indirectly discouraging the individual member's speech, did not abridge her free speech rights (*Phelan v. Laramie County Community College Board of Trustees*, 2000).

Newly elected board members often have little understanding of their actual role as individual board members. New member orientation (often provided by state school board associations) helps new members learn to become well informed on issues before voting, to abide by collective board decisions regardless of how he or she voted, and similar principles of "good boardsmanship." College staff members should provide extensive training to board members on issues that are particularly critical to the college. After a short period of learning and adjustment, most new board members will evolve into reasonably good team players who will work collegially with board colleagues to achieve the college's mission.

External Board Relations

The overriding principle governing external board relations is that the board speaks only as a whole. Individual board members should not attempt to speak for the board. When matters of public interest arise and it is likely that the media or civic groups will be asking for information from the board, one member should be designated to speak for the board. The remaining board members should refer all inquiries to the spokesperson. This avoids conflicting statements that can cause both legal and political problems for the board and allows the spokesperson to become thoroughly knowledgeable about the topic, resulting in accurate information being presented to the public.

Similarly, individual board members should not get involved in college business matters unless they have been expressly delegated specific authority to do so by the board. Well-meaning board members sometimes delve into college business on their own. For example, an individual board member looking at property for a new campus could drive up the price by alerting the owners of potential interest before the board itself has even considered the property. Board members should be discouraged from dealing with any outside entities unless express authority to do so has been granted by the board.

Board Member Liability

A frequent concern of board members, as well as top college administrators, is personal liability for actions taken in their official capacity in managing the college or district. Though on occasion a plaintiff will choose to sue individual board members, it is not common for individual members to be held personally liable. Most states provide a degree of immunity to board members for discretionary actions taken in good faith in the normal course of business. For example, two members of a Texas board were sued for defamation by a district superintendent after the board members discussed with the media their desire for an investigation of the superintendent's use of a district credit card. The court held that the two board members would be entitled to immunity for performance of a discretionary act if they conclusively established that their statements were made in good faith. The standard for federal civil rights actions under Section 1983 provides that a board member is entitled to qualified immunity unless it is shown that a reasonable person in his or her position, acting on his or her information and motivated by his or her purpose, would have known that the action taken by the board violated the clearly established rights of the plaintiff (*Hansen v. Bennett*, 1991). It is extremely rare, however, that a community college board member actually has to pay any portion of a judgment arising out of the college's operations. And if a board member is found liable, most states provide for indemnification of board members against liability stemming from actions taken by the board that were within the scope of their authority and taken in good faith, even if the action is later held to be legally incorrect.

Indemnification statutes are based on the policy that boards must be able to take action that is in the best interests of their institution without being overly concerned that personal liability could wipe out an individual member because of one action of the board. Similarly, nearly every institution will provide and pay for a legal defense for any board member who is named in a lawsuit as a result of actions taken by the board. The only exception to this principle occurs when a board member takes action in bad faith or maliciously, as when a member defames a member of the college community outside of a governing board meeting. Simply expressing personal animosity toward an individual outside of the board meeting context would generally be beyond the scope of a board member's duties and could result in personal liability that may not be indemnified.

Conflicts of Interest

A conflict of interest arises when a governing board member personally benefits from an action taken by the board. The law recognizes that an impairment of impartial judgment can occur in even the most well-meaning board members when their personal economic interests are affected by the business they transact on behalf of the public entity. Most states have specific regulations precluding such actions. Such regulations often include criminal penalties and vary from state to state in their scope. Consequently, each board member should become familiar with the scope of applicable state conflict-of-interest provisions.

Increasingly, the media and individual citizens are becoming more alert to conflicts of interests on the part of public officials. Political opponents of a board or an individual member will scrutinize board actions closely for any hint of conflict of interest. Particularly when contracts are awarded, board members should make certain that they will not personally benefit, either directly or indirectly, from the award of a contract to a particular party. In some cases, it is sufficient for a board member with a conflict of interest to withdraw from participating in discussion of the matter, abstain from voting, and disclose the personal interest. In other cases, the board may not take action at all (as in the case of a proposed contract between the community college and the board member himself, a spouse or close relative, or a company the member owns). An example of the latter occurred in the case of *Thorpe v. Long Beach Community College District* (2000), in which the husband of a longtime community college district accountant had been elected to the governing board. Because of her husband's board membership, the district refused to consider Thorpe for a promotion to a higher position, even though she had been employed by the district for twenty-two years before her husband became a board member. The court upheld the district's action, holding that the board member had a financial interest in his spouse's earnings, giving him a prohibited financial interest in any new contract of employment made by the board and his wife. The court noted that the purpose of the conflict-of-interest law is to ensure board members' absolute loyalty and undivided allegiance to the best interests of the government agency they serve and to remove all direct and indirect influence of a financially interested member. In light of recent corporate scandals, the public has become even more intolerant of officials who appear to be looking out for their own interests rather than those of the institution they serve. The college's legal counsel should be consulted if there appears to be any possibility of a conflict-of-interest issue, since the penalties are severe and the political repercussions for the board member are often substantial, even in minor conflict-of-interest cases.

Public Meetings

As a general rule, governing board business can be transacted only in formal board meetings. Every state has sunshine laws requiring that meetings of local government agencies, such as community college districts, be open to the public. All such open meeting laws have exceptions to the general rule that the public be allowed to attend the meeting. Though they vary from state to state, exceptions are usually provided for discussions of personnel matters, conferences with legal counsel concerning litigation, and matters such as the acquisition of real property.

Unfortunately, open meeting law litigation involving public institutions of higher education is common and has occurred in nearly all states. Although much of the litigation is brought by individuals who are strong proponents of "the public's right to know," all too often discretionary board decisions that cannot be attacked substantively are challenged as violations of public meeting laws, which often results in invalidation of the board action. For example, a high school football coach was able to overturn the termination of his coaching assignment simply by persuading the court that the school board failed to give him advance notice of the board meeting at which his coaching assignment had been terminated, pursuant to a statute requiring that employees be notified of meetings at which complaints against them will be heard (*Bell v. Vista Unified School District*, 2000). Consequently, it is extremely important for boards to be scrupulous in observing applicable open meeting laws. Since most board members are laypersons who do not have a clear knowledge of the applicable law, it is imperative that college leaders (especially the president) be familiar with open meeting laws to assist the board in achieving full compliance.

Invariably, governing boards face the problem of confidential information discussed in closed session being leaked to the media or interested parties by a board member. This seems to happen most commonly where a board member is closely aligned with a subset of college employees, such as faculty. Unfortunately, most state laws do not provide the remaining board members with effective remedies for such unprofessional action. Once again, the best technique to preclude such behavior is peer pressure from the board and the persuasion of all board members that the board should act as a team. Boards can and do censure offending board members when it is confirmed that they have leaked confidential information from closed sessions.

Board member training should include the potential for personal liability for board members who disclose confidential information. Individuals who are the subject of the unauthorized disclosure may be able to sue for defamation or invasion of privacy. Damages for invasion of privacy may be awarded even if the disclosure is true if it is the type of information that is damaging to the subject and is supposed to be kept confidential. In rare instances where a board member has repeatedly leaked confidential information to the detriment of the board or college, injunctive relief may be possible to order the misbehaving board member to cease and desist. However, this problem is rarely solved by legal means, leaving the personal approach as the only effective remedy.

In addition to the recurring issue of closed versus open meetings, boards must often deal with state statutes providing for public comment at board meetings. Public comment periods can be a significant tool for board members to stay in touch with the concerns of their constituents. In states not having such requirements, board policy often provides for public input at its meetings. Boards must honor these public comment requirements while maintaining the structure and effectiveness of their meetings. This can be difficult in the face of often difficult and verbose members of the public wishing to speak to the board. Reasonable time limits of three to five minutes for speakers have been upheld by the courts as long as the limits are applied consistently. In addition, speakers can be limited to matters within the board's jurisdiction or, if the board is considering a specific agenda item at the time, to that particular item. Speakers who are unduly repetitious or who veer off into an "extended discussion of irrelevancies" may be stopped (*White v. City of Norwalk*, 1990).

A more difficult problem arises when content-based issues arise, as when a speaker criticizes college employees or addresses an issue that is currently the subject of collective bargaining with the employee organization that represents the speaker. In an attempt to protect the privacy and reputation of college employees, some boards have tried to prohibit citizen speakers from criticizing employees in an open board meeting. Recent federal court decisions indicate that such efforts may violate speakers' constitutional rights. In one such case, a school board adopted a policy that prohibited "charges or complaints against any employee of the district, regardless of whether or not the employee is identified by name or by any reference which tends to identify the employee." The court found that the board meeting was a designated public forum and that compelling state interest was required in order to restrict speech based on content. The school district's argument that protection of the privacy interests of the employees and the board's interest in conducting an efficient, orderly meeting was rejected, and the prohibition against criticism of district employees was invalidated (*Baca v. Moreno Valley Unified School District* (1996). Similarly, policies that prohibit employees, or a class of employees such as teachers, from speaking to the board during a public comment period have also been ruled constitutionally invalid. This is true even where the comments relate to labor relations and the employees are represented by (but are not part of) an employee organization (*Madison Joint School District v. Wisconsin Employment Relations Commission*, 1976).

In summary, then, governing boards should be cautious about restricting speech during open public comment sessions of board meetings, except for uniformly applied time limits or commonsense limitations to subjects that are within the board's jurisdiction. Enforcement of content-based restrictions against speakers could result in board liability for deprivation of the speaker's clearly established constitutional rights. A helpful strategy to avoid public meeting attacks on staff is to have a complaint procedure whereby unhappy students or members of the public can attempt to resolve their concerns at a lower level, thereby precluding the need to air their grievances at a public board meeting. In any event, if a speaker begins to criticize the performance of a college employee, the board president should immediately offer the speaker an alternative means—such as a meeting with the appropriate college official—for airing his concerns. Alternatively, a college could hold "citizen's forum meetings" separate from board meetings, and guide citizens who want to publicly air their complaints to such sessions, which would have a lower profile than board meetings.

Public Records Issues

All fifty states have public records laws, many of which are based on the Federal Freedom of Information Act, which make most college records accessible for inspection by members of the public upon request. Standard exceptions are usually made for personnel records and attorney-client communications; however, documents withheld under public record laws may be obtained by subpoena if litigation arises. Consequently, staff and board members should consider carefully whether it is necessary to put in writing statements that are potentially adverse to the college's interests. Moreover, anything that is put in writing should be clear and accurate so that it is not easily distorted by individuals with adverse interests.

It may come as a surprise to many board members that these principles apply equally to e-mail messages. Under most states' public record acts, e-mail messages are as much subject to disclosure as messages on paper. While some messages to or from board members may be subject to various privileges from disclosure, board members should assume that their e-mail will become public and should avoid making any statement in an e-mail that is intended to be confidential.

Board Member Financial Responsibilities

The governing board is ultimately responsible for the financial well-being of the college. Boards carry out this responsibility by adopting the annual budget and monitoring revenue and expenses during the budget year.

Because there are multiple constituencies in the college—faculty, administrators, students—vying for available resources, the board must make difficult allocation choices while maintaining the quality of the institution. The actual supervision of expenditures is normally delegated to a myriad of college administrators, with very general board oversight. The board's most important responsibility here is to ensure that adequate controls are built into the budget-and-spend system. In addition, ensuring that the college has sound, practical policies and procedures—and that staff comply with them—will go a long way toward preventing litigation that can drain institutional financial resources.

The need for additional resources has led many institutions in recent years to create or expand private support groups and foundations whose goal is to raise additional funds for the college. Such entities are normally not subject to the same regulations as the college itself. This occasionally leads to injudicious use of funds for things such as luxury cars. Boards should closely monitor activities of any support organization using the college name, since any misconduct by the organization will reflect on the college's reputation.

Conclusion

Most of the problems that governing boards face can be dealt with successfully by providing board members with an appropriate level of education in the skills and legal precepts required for successful board membership. Training that emphasizes the fiduciary duty of board members for the academic and financial well-being of the institution should help overcome tendencies in decision making to favor one constituency over the institution's overall health. Specific training as to confidentiality, public access to information, and the public's rights in board meetings will preclude a great deal of expense and lost time that arises from legal challenges. And instruction in applicable conflict-of-interest rules will help board members recognize and avoid prohibited conflicts.

Legal References

Baca v. Moreno Valley Unified School District, 963 F.Supp. 719 (1996).
Bell v. Vista Unified School District, 82 Cal.App.4th 672 (2000).
Gabrilson v. Flynn, 554 N.W.2d 267 (Iowa 1996).
Hansen v. Bennett, 948 F.2d 397, 399 (7th Cir. 1991).
Madison Joint School District v. Wisconsin Employment Relations Commission 429 U.S. 167 (1976).
Phelan v. Laramie County Community College Board of Trustees, 235 F.3d 1243 (10th Cir. 2000).
State ex rel. Moore v. Brewster, 2003 WL 21738600 (July 29, 2003).
Thorpe v. Long Beach Community College District, 83 Cal.App.4th 655 (2000).
White v. City of Norwalk, 900 F.2d 1421 (9th Cir. 1990).

TIMOTHY K. GARFIELD *is a partner in the San Diego law firm of Stephenson, Worley, Garratt, Schwartz, Garfield & Prairie, specializing in education law.*

8

This chapter provides an overview of the risk
management process as applied to the community college.

Risk Management in the Community College Setting

Brett A. Sokolow

Risk management is essential for today's community colleges. Community colleges own buildings, land, and facilities; promote degrees and certifications in manifold disciplines; run campus and recreational activities; provide food service; offer benefits; own and operate vehicles, including mass transit; host public events; and manage human resources, among many other functions. Failure to assess operational risks and to address them constructively through risk management processes has left many colleges vulnerable to claims and lawsuits, stretching limited resources and draining contingency funds.

As the need for risk management has increased, so too has the sophistication of risk managers and the tools they can bring to bear on risks. What started in the 1970s as a certification program evolved into an academic major at some colleges, and now risk management is a field of study with students who receive degrees or professional certifications. Societies of risk managers now exist and have established professional ethics and standards of conduct. Risk management is essential for the multimillion-dollar operation that is today's community college.

It is necessary to say this because many colleges treat risk management as if it were optional or a fad. Relatively few colleges have risk management departments or even a professional risk manager, and this is especially true of community colleges. Yet nearly all corporations the size of colleges have professional risk managers, if not full-time risk management departments. Community colleges exist in a highly litigious society. Students are enrolling with more and more complex psychological and behavioral problems (Lake and Tribbensee, 2002). Insurance is getting more expensive, and insurance instruments are becoming more sophisticated. Although it is not necessary for every community college to employ a full-time risk management staff, it is essential that each college implement a risk management plan to protect institutional resources. This chapter provides practical advice for implementing effective risk management strategies in the community college.

The Risk Management Process

There are narrow and broad views of risk management. In the narrow view, the risk management function involves determining the insurance needs of the institution, bidding out insurance needs to brokers and purchasing necessary insurance, managing claims, and updating and renewing insurance coverage as necessary. This is a very narrow view of risk management because it focuses only on the insurance procurement aspect of a broader, more proactive process. On many college campuses, the risk manager is often someone with an insurance industry background who handles insurance procurement for the institution and little else. Often there is no full-time risk manager, and the institution's business officer or vice president for finance performs insurance-related functions. Yet there is much more to the process of risk management than the insurance procurement function.

This chapter views risk management as a process rather than simply an insurance-related function. This broad view of risk management identifies a four-step process: assess risk for the operations of the institution, prioritize the risks, address the risks, and evaluate the efficacy of the methods chosen to address the risks. The process is continuous because after evaluation, the process begins all over again as time and variables change, thereby creating the necessity to reassess the risks and repeat the four steps to keep current. This four-step process is the true essence of risk management.

Assessing Risk for the Operations of the Institution. Inherent in the operation of a college is the facilitation of activities that engender risk at varying levels (Bickel and Lake, 1999). This is by no means bad. All colleges engage in certain risks associated with normal day-to-day functions of a community college, such as the transportation of students, food preparation and service, and the operation of mechanical equipment, such as boilers, kilns, landscaping machines, and lathes. Some colleges engender higher risks by sponsoring programs that are more physically hazardous, such as training for careers in mechanical fields. Whenever risk is present, it must be addressed effectively and assessed accurately. Correctly done, risk assessment is a formalized, intentional process. However, many institutions fail to recognize a risk until they are sued for it.

Because community colleges rarely employ a full-time risk management team, centralized comprehensive risk assessment operations are not possible. One of the most useful alternative techniques employed by effective risk managers is to train department heads to function as risk managers for their own departments. This method is efficient and works well because department heads are typically very familiar with the operations and risks associated with their departmental activities. The assessment role of the administrative risk manager involves the following activities:

- Determining the training competencies for the department heads
- Creating the training schedule
- Providing the actual training
- Providing the department heads with support materials
- Establishing timetables for completing the departmental assessments
- Providing instructions for department heads on how to seek assistance, if needed
- Establishing in what form the assessments should be submitted and how they should be submitted

The first step in the training is to have each department head complete a thorough list of all the operations within that department. Once each department has submitted a list, the administrative risk manager may need to make some decisions about how thorough the assessment can or should be. Rotational assessments can be useful. Perhaps half the list of one department will be addressed in the fall semester and the second half in the spring. Or certain items may be assessed in the coming year while others are postponed for a future year.

A mechanism should also be created for deciding how dispersed the assessment process should be. If a department head oversees fifteen different operations, it may be necessary to provide training department by department until each individual responsible for an operation becomes the assessor for and risk manager of the operation. For example, in the wake of the Texas Aggie Bonfire tragedy, Texas A&M University decided it wanted to have tighter control and more oversight of the activities of its student organizations. With more than seven hundred different recognized student organizations, there was no way for the university's risk managers to oversee the activities of all of them. Texas A&M created a risk management division within student activities and set about training the officers and advisers of each of these seven hundred organizations to become the risk management deputies for their respective organizations. Each organization conducted an audit of its activities, engaged in an assessment process, and came to the student activities risk management division with a strategic plan to address its risks. The new student activities–based risk management system has been implemented, to spectacular effect.[1] Although community colleges never experience such a concentration of student organizations, the community aspects of the college setting, including student clubs and organizations, are receiving more emphasis and more participation from students, and that may entail elevated risks.

Uniform Assessment Methods and Criteria. It is important to use a unified risk assessment system institutionwide, rather than having multiple systems in different departments. The simplest system to use is a three-category assessment: low risk, moderate risk, and high risk. A system using three classifications is less complex than more multivariate approaches and therefore easier to implement because it uses fairly subjective, large classes rather than objectively defined cutoffs, such as property value or potential financial loss. Criteria should be established for each category that can subjectively address institutional risk tolerances.

Often insurers and brokers offer basic assessment tools that can be used with this approach. While suitable for some institutions, one of these may be too blunt an instrument for others. Some risk assessments use a color-keyed, multicategory scheme not unlike the Homeland Security Advisory System: low (green), guarded (blue), elevated (yellow), high (orange), severe (red). The most sophisticated risk assessments are algorithmic or multivariate systems that assess risk on the basis of input from the department head, national insurance data, similar institutions, geographical litigation trends, and other sources. These can be plotted and graphed on risk maps. Risk mapping is becoming more and more useful and relevant as technology progresses. One of the best-known and most effective mapping systems is the threat assessment MOSAIC developed by Gavin de Becker & Associates.[2] The best approach is to start with a simple system and become more sophisticated as necessary.

Risk assessments take time. It is unlikely that a thorough assessment of the operations of a community college can be completed in one year. Many administrative risk managers find it useful to create a multiyear assessment plan, keeping department heads on a rotating schedule that is prioritized by the risk manager.

Prioritizing the Risks. This second step in the risk management process could be as simple as collecting all of the high-risk items from the assessments completed by the department heads and deciding to work on those for the current academic year. Or the risk manager might decide to take all of those high-risk items and then prioritize within that list, identifying items of greater or lesser criticality. Criticality is subjective because it is dependent on institutional priorities. Criticality might be measured by risk of death and injury, by financial losses, by reputational losses, by whether the risk is part of an essential function or is tangential, and many other factors. A more sophisticated format would allow the risk manager to blend high and moderate risks into groupings, such as the case where a high risk from one department and a high or moderate risk from another department are strategically similar and can be dealt with more easily together. The most sophisticated assessments take the rating of each risk and then organize them according to the severity and type of the risk. Each of the following five types of risk can add another layer to the prioritization process.

Strategic Risks. Strategic risks relate to the objectives and goals of the institutional mission. These types of risk tend to be more intangible than other types. For example, a working farm adjacent to the community college might be put up for sale. The question might arise as to whether the community college should try to acquire the property. Strategic risks examine this decision, considering factors such as what the farm might be used for if acquired by a party other than the college. An industrial plant next door might adversely affect the college, and so a decision to purchase the farm might be advantageous, depending on zoning regulations and site improvement potentialities. Would owning the farm support the institution's expansion strategy by providing a venue for an expanded agricultural program or more land for needed campus buildings and facilities? Strategic risks relate to the operational infrastructure of the institution and whether that infrastructure supports the objectives and goals. Strategic risks are risk factors that have the potential to affect the strategic goals of the institution.

Reputational Risk. Reputational risk is less tangible. Institutions build reputations over many years and are rightly protective of their name and image. Risk management can control some exposure to events that could tarnish the institution's reputation. Risk managers can sharpen the standards and the policies that public relations personnel use to guide their communications and advise on potential legal ramifications to public statements. It might be easy to grasp this type of risk if you asked what your community college is known for. Is it turning out great marketers, offering a solid computer technology department, or developing a well-regarded transfer program? If something were to tarnish the shine on that department or program, how might your college suffer in attracting students to that program or lose prestige or recognition for the excellence of the program?

Financial Risk. Financial risks to the institution take the form of civil legal actions such as misrepresentation and defamation, violations of law such as copyright or trademark infringement, contractual claims, First Amendment violations, and the monetary risks inherent in ownership of real estate, vehicles, and other property. For example, if colleges do not take proactive steps to educate drivers on the safe operation of college-owned vans and other vehicles, in the event of an accident, the college could be liable in a negligence suit for subjecting passengers or bystanders to a foreseeable risk of bodily harm.

Operational Risk. Operational risks arise from personnel management decisions, the provision of health and medical services, campus safety, outside groups using institutional facilities, sports teams, classroom activities, study abroad, and many other activities. A prime example might be a student in a cooperative program who travels twice a week to an off-campus vocational training site selected by the community college. Is the site safe? Could the college be held liable for assigning a student to an unsafe, hazardous, or crime-ridden environment without adequate warning to the student?

Compliance Risk. Federal and state governments have given colleges a myriad of complicated, conflicting, confounding, and overlapping regulations and laws by which administrators must abide. Who is ensuring that regulations are met and laws are complied with accurately? If an interpretation of law is needed, where is it to be found?

Addressing the Risk. If prioritizing the risk sounds complicated, the next step, addressing the risk, should seem easier because there are only three things that administrators can do with risk: risk can be avoided; risk can be transferred; or risk can be accepted. Some risk managers add risk retention as a separate category, but this chapter presents risk retention as a subset of risk acceptance.

Risk Avoidance. The first thing that administrators can do with risk is avoid it. Avoiding risk is not always the most desirable or best option, but it is a useful tool when appropriate. The skilled risk manager knows when to say no. For example, the Texas Aggies will not be having a bonfire of the same scale and construction anytime soon. Risk avoidance should be practiced under three circumstances: when the risk cannot be transferred adequately, when the risk cannot be sufficiently or cost-effectively insured, or when the risk of loss is so high that the activity or operation is simply not acceptable.

Risk Transfer. Risk transfer means that some or all of the risk is shifted to another party. A classic example is a group or organization that wants to host a cocktail reception on campus. If members of the group obtain and serve the cocktails, the group and the institution share all risk. If a licensed outside vendor is hired to serve alcohol at the party, some risk will be transferred to the vendor, though some risk will also likely remain with the group and the institution. If the party is hosted off campus at a site controlled by the outside vendor and that vendor controls all aspects of alcohol service, it is likely that all risk will be transferred to the vendor. Various risk transfer strategies are available to community college leaders, and policies, brochures, and open communications from departments to risk management about operational activities can help ensure that risk is transferred wherever possible and whenever appropriate.

Risk Acceptance. Risk acceptance is practiced whenever a risk is so low that it is nominal or acceptable. Community colleges often have far more vehicular traffic than four-year colleges because most students commute, whereas many four-year colleges ban cars for first-year and often second-year students. More traffic on campus increases the risk of car theft, pedestrian injury, and collisions. Yet we accept that commuters need cars, and we accordingly accept their presence and the risk that follows. Risk acceptance is also applicable to moderate-risk and high-risk activities and operations. When a decision is made to accept risk, a decision is also usually made to insure for it so that the institution does not bear the sole risk of loss. Insuring a loss can also be described as having the same impact as partial risk transfer, although with insurance it is not the risk but the loss that is transferred. This is where the insurance procurement mentioned at the beginning of this chapter can enter into the picture as a risk management function. Where a risk is assessed and then prioritized and a decision is made to accept it, insurance is then procured to cover any potential losses related to that risk.

As noted earlier, some people consider risk retention one of the acceptable options for contending with risk. Yet risk retention is just a form of insurance. Consider that insurance is not a complete shifting of loss. For any insured loss, there is a deductible paid by the insured. When we insure something, we agree to pay some portion of our own loss in order to keep our premiums manageable. This is also called a retained limit. Risk retention often results in a very high deductible, thereby retaining a greater portion of the potential loss by the insured in order to reduce premiums. For many community colleges, a risk retention program has been a tremendous boon, with the institution often assuming self-insurance up to $100,000 or more, even into the millions of dollars in some cases. This is beneficial because it lowers premiums and sometimes reduces the need to make claims, thereby reducing premium increases that might result from a series of claims on which the insurer has to pay.

Evaluating the Efficacy of the Methods Chosen to Address the Risks. This is the last step of the four-step risk management process. Once risk has been assessed, prioritized, and addressed, it is important to make sure on a continuing basis that you have appropriately applied the first three steps. For example, a complex accountability scheme for lab safety, food service employees, or ergonomics in compliance with occupational health and safety regulations may be rendered useless if the law that the scheme was designed to address is changed, overturned by a court, or otherwise altered. Risk managers may then reduce that risk from moderate to low and respond accordingly, assuming that the risk is compliance-based and there are no reasons to maintain the risk level outside of the regulatory requirement. However, a situation may still be dangerous even if the law requiring you to make it safer is repealed. The insightful risk manager is always trying to keep abreast of campus events, plans, and changes.

Practical Application of Risk Management Philosophy

This section of the chapter looks forward, anticipating the high-risk issues and litigation trends community colleges will be facing in student affairs and student conduct issues to prepare leaders for proactive management of future risk. Examples applying the broad risk management ideas described in this chapter are offered here with an emphasis on issues related to student affairs.

Assessing the Risk. Student affairs, student development, and student conduct are becoming more important to the community college as students demand higher levels of service and concurrently display conduct that requires more attention. Student-focused activities are giving rise to greater levels of dollar liability and potential reputational harm. Risk managers may have a well-established student affairs department, be instituting one, or just have a need for one—but at any stage, the relevance of risk assessment to student affairs is clear. To be proactive, we must ask questions about operations, claims, litigation, and other risk factors, such as the following (Sokolow, 2002):

- What kinds of student-affairs activities pose higher risks? Is the trend toward greater student affairs–related liability inevitable?
- Are college policies and practices exacerbating risk in any way?
- Is there anything that can be done to counter the trend toward increasing risk?
- Can risks be minimized through avoidance, transfer, policies, practices, procedures, or insurance?
- Can risks be minimized without compromising student affairs goals and objectives?
- Can risk be reduced by focusing on issues such as hazing, drinking, eating disorders, and sexual assault?

Prioritizing the Risk. In risk management, it is essential to prioritize the various risks to the institution. To facilitate this process, administrators should consider questions such as the following: Is the student affairs department being sued? How often? What for? What are the trends, if any?

Do policies promote student safety and encourage aggrieved students to seek relief through the institution, or are they turning first to lawyers? Does the college have clear policies on issues such as sexual assault and sexual harassment? Are reporting procedures detailed and useful? Are staff members trained properly?

How does your institution address coercive lawsuits? Students today are threatening to sue—and suing—on baseless grievances. They know that colleges are image-conscious and that some institutions will settle a baseless claim rather than dispute it. Will your community college address this issue on a case-by-case basis, or will it follow the example of some colleges that have let it be known that they will not be coerced into settling frivolous suits?

Is your college being sued as a result of judicial hearing outcomes? If so, are you winning or losing? When your college is being sued or initiating settlement talks in lieu of suit, are the threats of litigation coming more often from victims of those who violate campus conduct codes or the accused perpetrators? Do the victims' grievances come from the injuries they sustained or from the college's handling of the complaint?

Is your college studying student safety regularly? Why spend on drug programming if alcohol is the drug of choice for your students (or vice versa)? If risk is not measured, you are just guessing. Simple surveys about student involvement in high-risk activities can help community college administrators stay up-to-date on student behaviors. Anecdotal information and assumptions can lead to inefficient resource allocation. Do not base assessment solely on judicial cases because many severe incidents are never reported to campus authorities. For example, studies have noted that fewer than 10 percent of sexual assault victims report their victimizations to authorities (Koss, Gidycz, and Wisniewski, 1987). A survey of students, over time, can provide much clearer indications on student safety issues and trends (Sokolow, 2002).

The questions listed here are examples. You can and should be asking similar questions about student health services, campus law enforcement, externships, and any other divisional responsibilities that fall under student affairs at the college.

Addressing the Risks. Once you have assessed and prioritized all of the varied risks, you are ready to address them. Look at the answers to the thoughtful questions you have asked. Suppose that your college has a fledgling student conduct system and it is clear that the judicial staff needs additional training and development. Perhaps the risk manager can have a hand in securing resources or trainers. At the same time, the risk manager may find it prudent to increase coverage for the administrators under the "trustees and officers" policy or the "errors and omissions" policy. Occasionally, it is determined that the contract security firm is not meeting the safety needs of students on campus. If so, it may be necessary to create a campus police department staffed by full-time certified officers.

Evaluating the Efficacy of the Methods Chosen to Address the Risks. Once you have taken concrete steps to address risk through modification of policies, procedures, practices, and insurance coverage, you should initiate an evaluation process to ensure that the steps you have taken are adequately serving the needs you intended them to serve. If an academic building on campus has suffered a rash of break-ins at night, you might step up night patrols of the building, only to find that the break-in pattern switches to a more daring daylight mode or to another building entirely. You will need to shift your plan to address the changing crime pattern.

Conclusion

The aims of this chapter have been to provide an overview of the risk management process as applied to the community college setting and to present practical examples of applications of that process. I hope you have found pieces of information that will be helpful to you as you strive to deploy effective risk management strategies at your community college.

Notes

1. For more information, go to the Texas A&M Web site [http://studentactivities.tamu.edu/risk].
2. For details, go to the Gavin de Becker Web site [http://www.gdbinc.com/MOSAIC].

References

Bickel, R., and Lake, P. *The Rights and Responsibilities of the Modern University.* Durham, N.C.: Carolina Academic Press, 1999.

Koss, M. P., Gidycz, C. A., and Wisniewski, N. "The Scope of Rape: Incidence and Prevalence of Sexual Aggression and Victimization in a National Sample of Higher Education Students." *Journal of Consulting and Clinical Psychology,* 1987, 55, 162–170.

Lake, P. F., and Tribbensee, N. "The Emerging Crisis of College Student Suicide: Law and Policy Responses to Serious Forms of Self-Inflicted Injury." *Stetson Law Review,* 2002, 32.

Sokolow, B. A. "Risk Assessment in Student Affairs." In B. Sokolow (ed.), *Instilling Principles of Risk Management into the Daily Practice of Student Affairs.* Radnor, Pa.: NCHERM/URMIA, 2002.

BRETT A. SOKOLOW, J.D., *is a higher education attorney and risk management consultant. He is president of the National Center for Higher Education Risk Management (http://www.ncherm.org) in Pennsylvania.*

9

This chapter provides a description of additional resources on legal issues at community colleges.

Legal Resources for Community Colleges

Carol A. Kozeracki

This chapter provides information about Internet search strategies for legal case references as well as a bibliography of books and ERIC documents with additional information on issues addressed in this volume. Also included are listings of organizations that address higher education legal issues, some of which are primarily for lawyers and some of which are for administrators who deal with legal issues.

Internet Search Strategies for Case References

LexisNexis: http://web.lexis-nexis.com/universe

This fee-based service allows you to do research using case law, secondary literature, and federal and state codes. Access this service from a library or university that subscribes to the service. Search for legal decisions either by party name or case citation by going to the main Web site and clicking on "Legal Research" and "Get a Case." For example, in Chapter Seven of this volume, Timothy Garfield refers to the case of *White v. City of Norwalk*, which he cites in the references as "*White v. City of Norwalk*, 900 F.2d 1421 (9th Cir. 1990)." You can either enter "White" and "City of Norwalk" as the two party names, or you can enter "900 F.2d 1421" as the citation. Click on the link "View Citation Formats" to make sure you're following the proper protocol. Using party names brings up all related cases, including prior decisions and appeals, whereas using the citation will bring up information on the specific decision.

FindLaw: http://www.findlaw.com/casecode
    This free service allows you to search Supreme Court cases back to 1893 and U.S. Court of Appeals cases back to the mid-1990s. It also provides links to U.S. trial court Web sites and to U.S. state cases, codes, statutes, and regulations. Cases can be searched by citation number, party name, or full text.

Organizations That Address Legal Issues in Higher Education

American Association of University Professors: http://www.aaup.org/Legal/index.htm
    The AAUP has a legal office with expertise in academic freedom, discrimination, affirmative action, and faculty contract. Online materials available in full text through the Web site include "Informational Outlines" that provide understandable interpretations of court findings in areas such as domestic partnership benefits, student grades, distance learning, and intellectual property. The site also offers an "Annual Legal Update: 'Hot' Topics in Higher Education Law."

Council on Law in Higher Education: http://www.clhe.org
    The CLHE is a national organization that educates and informs education administrators and policymakers about the leading law and policy issues affecting the higher education system. CLHE members receive comprehensive law and policy updates, best practices briefs, discounts on educational programs and books, public policy reports, easy-to-understand compliance information, and detailed analyses of pending and recent legislation, regulations, and case law.

Education Law Association: http://www.educationlaw.org
    The ELA is a nonprofit, nonadvocacy organization that promotes interest in and understanding of the legal framework of education and the rights of students, parents, school boards, and school employees. It produces a series of monographs and books and publishes an annual yearbook that analyzes the previous year's federal and state court decisions affecting public and private education.

National Association of College and University Attorneys: http://www.nacua.org
    The NACUA is the central organization for higher education legal counsel. Its main mission is to advance the effective practice of higher education attorneys for the benefit of the colleges and universities they serve. A series of publications can be ordered online at http://www.nacua.org/publications/pubsonline.html. Of special interest are the low-cost pamphlets, which are targeted to administrators and faculty, as well as legal counsel.

They address topics such as "Defamation Issues in Higher Education," "The Family Educational Rights and Privacy Act: A General Overview," and "Accommodating Faculty and Staff with Psychiatric Disabilities." Discounts are available to anyone at a college that has a membership in NACUA. A list of members is available at www.nacua.org/membership/institutions.asp.

Legal Books for the Layperson

Braxton, J. M., and Bayer, A. E. *Faculty Misconduct in Collegiate Teaching.* Baltimore: Johns Hopkins University Press, 1999.

Based on a study of faculty who teach undergraduate courses at different higher education institutions, this book looks at the influence of discipline and institution on norms of professorial behavior. The authors conclude that teaching norms are informally defined and observed and argue that a formal code of ethics for undergraduate teaching would serve the purpose of improving undergraduate education and elevating the status of college teaching.

Gordon, M., and Keiser, S. (eds.). *Accommodations in Higher Education Under the Americans with Disabilities Act: A No-Nonsense Guide for Clinicians, Educators, Administrators, and Lawyers.* New York: Guilford Press, 1998.

This book outlines some general foundational principles of the ADA, including its identification as a civil rights act and not an entitlement program.

Hendrickson, R. M. *The Colleges, Their Constituencies, and the Courts.* (2nd ed.) Dayton, Ohio: Education Law Association, 1999.

This book provides some background information on judicial review, federalism and the Bill of Rights, the legal development of public and private higher education, and the application of the state action doctrine to private higher education, as well as the evolving relationship between higher education corporations and their various constituencies.

Kaplin, W. A., and Lee, B. A. *The Law of Higher Education: A Comprehensive Guide to Legal Implications of Administrative Decision Making.* (3rd ed.) San Francisco: Jossey-Bass, 1995.

This volume on higher education law is probably the best-known resource in the field and covers the following nine major areas: overview of postsecondary education law; the college and trustees, administrators, and staff; the college and the faculty; the college and the students; the college and the community; the college and the state government; the college and the federal government; the college and the education associations; and the college and the business and industrial community. Each chapter uses existing case law to describe the important issues on the topic and concludes with an annotated bibliography of related sources. Case, statute, and subject indexes are at the back of the book. An instructional supplement is available for individuals using *The Law of Higher Education* as a course text as well as an adaptation of the third edition that focuses on legal issues faced by student affairs professionals.

Olivas, M. *The Law and Higher Education: Cases and Materials on Colleges in Court.* (2nd ed.) Durham, N.C.: Carolina Academic Press, 1997.

This book reflects the extraordinary growth in the law of higher education and the accompanying rise in scholarship and commentary on higher education law and governance. The second edition includes new treatment of all areas, especially academic freedom, sexual and racial harassment issues, the gender and racial composition of colleges, tenure and denial of tenure, religion on campus, affirmative action, and the continuing development of due process for student on campus. A sixty-four-page 2003 supplement to this book is available.

Poskanzer, S. G. *Higher Education Law: The Faculty.* Baltimore: Johns Hopkins University Press, 2001.

This book was written to help faculty and administrators navigate critical legal issues and avoid potential legal pitfalls. It defines the central legal principles governing the activities of faculty and the routine academic affairs of colleges and universities. The major sections of the book cover the law relating to faculty as scholars, teachers, institutional citizens, public citizens, and employees.

Redfield, S. E. *Thinking Like a Lawyer: An Educator's Guide to Legal Analysis and Research.* Durham, N.C.: Carolina Academic Press, 2002.

This book provides a bridge between the legal professional and the education professional, offering an introduction to legal analysis using narrative, court cases, study tips, research methodologies, and an extensive glossary. Topics include information on how to read and understand case law and how to conduct legal research.

Thomas, S. B. *Students, Colleges, and Disability Law.* Dayton, Ohio: Education Law Association, 2002.

This book reviews disability laws in detail, as well as the roles of staff within a student disability services unit, the nature of mental and physical disabilities and how they are assessed, student admission and financial aid, reasonable and unreasonable accommodation, student records, and employment discrimination.

Toma, J. D., and Palm, R. L. *The Academic Administrator and the Law: What Every Dean and Department Chair Needs to Know* (ASHE-ERIC Higher Education Report Vol. 26, No. 5). Washington, D.C.: Graduate School of Education and Human Development, George Washington University, 1999.

This book synthesizes the research literature on legal issues that school deans and department chairs face as they perform their many duties. It pays particular attention to contract and tort matters for staff and students, constitutional and statutory due process, equal protection, free expression, and external regulations in areas such as immigration and copyright. It also defines the role of the institutional counsel and explains the litigation process.

Relevant ERIC Documents

Academic Senate for California Community Colleges. *Academic Freedom and Tenure: A Faculty Perspective.* Sacramento, Calif.: Academic Senate for California Community Colleges, 1999. (ED421189)

This publication presents the Academic Senate for California Community Colleges' position in support of academic freedom and tenure. It includes a brief history of academic freedom in the United States, highlighting the American Association of University Professors' fundamental policy statement from 1940. Statements attacking academic freedom and tenure are quoted, and the special situation of part-time and contract faculty is discussed within the context of academic freedom. The publication includes an annotated bibliography of resource materials on academic freedom and tenure and four appendixes of selected academic freedom and tenure policy statements and resolutions.

Cloud, R. C. "The New York Times Rule in Higher Education." *Education Law Reporter, 166*(1), 1–29, Aug. 15, 2002.

Executive administrators are vulnerable to the malice and defamatory attacks of critics on and off their campuses. This article documents the impact of the actual malice standard on public higher education administrators since the U.S. Supreme Court's 1964 decision in *New York Times Co. v. Sullivan* and reviews that case and twenty-three related state and federal cases.

Demac, D. "Campus Copyright Controversy: Who Really Owns Digital Course Material?" *Community College Journal,* 1998, *69*(1), 20–23.

This article analyzes the conflict between faculty and institutions over ownership of digital curricular materials. It suggests that colleges consult with faculty to develop policies for allocating ownership and licensing rights in a way that allows all to benefit.

Findlen, G. L. "Aspects of Difficult Decisions." In D. Robillard Jr. (ed.), *Dimensions of Managing Academic Affairs in the Community College.* New Directions for Community Colleges, no. 109. San Francisco: Jossey-Bass, 2000. (ED440697)

This chapter outlines five aspects that deans should consider when making sensitive, difficult decisions: problems, issues, players, options, and principles.

Haston, C. "Enlightening Chairs and Deans About Liability: How to Avoid Employment Litigation." In *The Olympics of Leadership: Overcoming Obstacles, Balancing Skills, Taking Risks*. Proceeding of the Annual International Conference of the National Community College Chair Academy, Phoenix, Ariz., 1996. (ED394563)

In addition to organizational liability, deans and department chairs can be held personally liable for their actions in certain circumstances. Personnel decisions and sexual harassment complaints are two areas where deans and department chairs must act thoughtfully and carefully to avoid possible liability. Strategies are provided for properly addressing complaints and avoiding litigation in these areas.

Kater, S., and Levin, J. S. "Shared Governance in Community Colleges in the Global Economy." Paper presented at the annual meeting of the American Educational Research Association, New Orleans, Apr. 2002. (ED465396)

This study consisted of document analysis of 237 collective bargaining agreements representing faculty at 301 community colleges in twenty-two states. Documents were analyzed and coded, and sixteen governance areas were identified, including budget, calendar, curriculum, discipline, evaluation, and tenure. This study indicates that centralization of decision making through collective bargaining has not limited faculty in their participation in governance but rather through contractual agreements has expanded their influence and participation. Economizing behaviors, represented by faculty participation in governance, are evident in community colleges and are consistent with their integration into the global economy.

Lau, R. *Employment Rights of Administrators in the California Community Colleges*. Unpublished manuscript, 1997. (ED405925)

This document discusses the rights of community college administrators to continued employment and the related obligations of college districts. Key elements of employment law are described in relation to provisions in the First and Fourteenth Amendments to the U.S. Constitution, due process, issues of discrimination, and necessary components of employment contracts. Other sections discuss the impact of the California Education Code, the California Code of Regulations, and local district boards. Fourteen court cases involving employment disputes are reviewed, and recommendations for improving employment practices are provided.

McIsaac, M. S., and Rowe, J. "Ownership and Access: Copyright and Intellectual Property in the On-Line Environment." In C. L. Dillon and R.

Cintrón (eds.), *Building a Working Policy for Distance Education.* New Directions for Community Colleges, no. 99. San Francisco: Jossey-Bass, 1997. (EJ554315)

This chapter argues that community colleges must address four major issues regarding intellectual property and the development of Internet course materials: copyright, fair use, duplication, and revenue generation for print and nonprint educational materials. It suggests that intellectual property issues be viewed as a continuum from low to high levels of risk.

Rafes, R., and Warren, E. "Hiring and Firing in Community Colleges: Caveats and Considerations for Protecting Institutions and Employees." *Community College Journal of Research and Practice,* 2001, 25(4), 283–296.

This article discusses the hiring and firing process in community colleges, including job posting, advertising positions, screening applicants, interviewing, testing, checking references, and making a job offer. It also explains the most effective ways to discipline and terminate employees, in keeping with employment laws.

Requirements of the Copyright Laws as They Apply to Higher Education. Salt Lake City, Utah: Salt Lake Community College Administrative Services, 1999. (ED447873)

This handbook provides guidelines for members of the Salt Lake Community College community, faculty, administrators, staff, and students in using copyrighted materials legally and appropriately. Except where copying without permission is specifically given in this handbook, prior written permission must be obtained from the copyright owner for use of any portion of copyrighted material.

Romas, T., and Parmer, H. "Workplace Violence, Hate Crimes, and Free Speech: A Proactive Approach." Paper presented at the annual chancellor's conference of the California Community Colleges, San Jose, Mar. 1996. (ED394532)

In any threat management effort, it is important that a proactive approach be taken and that individuals not try simply to ignore potentially violent situations. In addition, campuses should develop a policy and plan for all employees to help them recognize and respond to workplace violence. Recommended emergency response procedures are included. A sample board policy and regulations for workplace violence are appended.

Sandmann, W. "It's Still All Right to Complain (At Least for the Moment): Vincennes University and the Angry Professors." Paper presented at the annual meeting of the National Communication Association, Atlanta, Nov. 2001. (ED461134)

This paper focuses on an allegation that three faculty members of Vincennes University, a two-year school in Indiana, were denied merit raises because they had complained about how Vincennes treated its faculty. The paper briefly discusses the relevant facts of the case, analyzes the ruling of the court as it affects academic freedom and freedom of expression, contrasts and compares this case with some other cases, and discusses the implications that this case and other cases may have on academic freedom and freedom of expression. This brief analysis suggests that there appears to be decreasing support for academic freedom, both legally and rhetorically.

Smith, S. G. *"Cohen v. San Bernardino Valley College:* The Scope of Academic Freedom Within the Context of Sexual Harassment Claims and In-Class Speech." *Journal of College and University Law,* 1998, 25(1), 1–51.
    This article examines the issue of a professor's First Amendment right to academic freedom versus a student's right to an effective learning environment free from sexual harassment as set forth in *Cohen v. San Bernardino Valley College* (1996). Also explored is the right of a public employee to free speech. Recommendations are offered to college administrators on balancing competing policy interests.

Woolley, R. and others. *A Leadership Imperative: Addressing Legal Issues.* Unpublished manuscript, 1995. (ED388335)
    This document discusses legal issues for student development personnel not engaged in instruction and therefore falling outside of traditional academic rulings. Topics addressed include First Amendment issues in the context of an academic environment, highlighting decisions in cases where the right to freedom of expression and association on campus and via e-mail conflicted with respect for racial, ethnic, and religious groups. Other sections discuss judicial issues related to student disciplinary action, due process for students, regulation of off-campus conduct, disciplinary counseling, and procedures of referral and efficient withdrawal of students suffering from psychiatric disorders.

CAROL A. KOZERACKI is assistant director of the Institute for the Study of Educational Entrepreneurship, a partnership between the Graduate School of Education and Information Studies and the Anderson School at UCLA.

Index

Back Issue/Subscription Order Form

Copy or detach and send to:
Jossey-Bass, A Wiley Imprint, 989 Market Street, San Francisco CA 94103-1741

Call or fax toll-free: Phone 888-378-2537 6:30AM – 3PM PST; Fax 888-481-2665

Back Issues: Please send me the following issues at $29 each
(Important: please include ISBN number with your order.)

_____

_____

_____

$ _____ Total for single issues

$ _____ SHIPPING CHARGES: SURFACE   Domestic Canadian
                                             First Item $5.00 $6.00
                                      Each Add'l Item $3.00 $1.50
For next-day and second-day delivery rates, call the number listed above.

Subscriptions Please __ start __ renew my subscription to *New Directions for Community Colleges* for the year 2____ at the following rate:

U.S.	__ Individual $80	__ Institutional $165
Canada	__ Individual $80	__ Institutional $165
All Others	__ Individual $104	__ Institutional $239
Online Subscription		__ Institutional $165

**For more information about online subscriptions visit
www.interscience.wiley.com**

$ _____ Total single issues and subscriptions (Add appropriate sales tax for your state for single issue orders. No sales tax for U.S. subscriptions. Canadian residents, add GST for subscriptions and single issues.)

__Payment enclosed (U.S. check or money order only)
__VISA __ MC __ AmEx __ # _____ Exp. Date _____

Signature _____ Day Phone _____
__ Bill Me (U.S. institutional orders only. Purchase order required.)

Purchase order # _____
           Federal Tax ID13559302   **GST 89102 8052**

Name _____

Address _____

_____

Phone _____ E-mail _____

For more information about Jossey-Bass, visit our Web site at www.joss eybass.com

CC119 **Developing Successful Partnerships with Business and the Community**
Mary S. Spangler
Demonstrates that there are many different approaches to community
colleges' partnering with the private sector and that when partners are
actively engaged in tailoring education, training, and learning to their
students, everyone is the beneficiary.
ISBN: 0-7879-6321-9

CC118 **Community College Faculty: Characteristics, Practices, and Challenges**
Charles Outcalt
Offers multiple perspectives on the ways community college faculty fulfill
their complex professional roles. With data from national surveys, this
volume provides an overview of community college faculty, looks at their
primary teaching responsibility, and examines particular groups of
instructors, including part-timers, women, and people of color.
ISBN: 0-7879-6328-3

CC117 **Next Steps for the Community College**
Trudy H. Bers, Harriott D. Calhoun
Provides an overview of relevant literature and practice covering major
community college topics: transfer rates, vocational education, remedial
and developmental education, English as a second language education,
assessment of student learning, student services, faculty and staff, and
governance and policy. Includes a chapter discussing the categories,
types, and purposes of literature about community colleges and the
major publications germane to community college practitioners and
scholars.
ISBN: 0-7879-6289-9

CC116 **The Community College Role in Welfare to Work**
C. David Lisman
Provides examples of effective programs including a job placement program
meeting the needs of rural welfare recipients, short-term and advanced levels
of technical training, a call center program for customer service job training,
beneficial postsecondary training, collaborative programs for long-term
family economic self-sufficiency, and a family-based approach recognizing
the needs of welfare recipients and their families.
ISBN: 0-7879-5781-X

CC115 **The New Vocationalism in Community Colleges**
Debra D. Bragg
Analyzes the role of community college leaders in developing programs,
successful partnerships and collaboration with communities, work-based
learning, changes in perception of terminal education and transfer
education, changing instructional practices for changing student populations
and the integration of vocational education into the broader agenda of
American higher education.
ISBN: 0-7879-5780-1

**NEW DIRECTIONS FOR COMMUNITY COLLEGES
IS NOW AVAILABLE ONLINE AT WILEY INTERSCIENCE**

What is Wiley InterScience?

Wiley InterScience is the dynamic online content service from John Wiley & Sons delivering the full text of over 300 leading scientific, technical, medical, and professional journals, plus major reference works, the acclaimed *Current Protocols* laboratory manuals, and even the full text of select Wiley print books online.

What are some special features of Wiley InterScience?

Wiley InterScience Alerts is a service that delivers table of contents via e-mail for any journal available on Wiley InterScience as soon as a new issue is published online.
Early View is Wiley's exclusive service presenting individual articles online as soon as they are ready, even before the release of the compiled print issue. These articles are complete, peer-reviewed, and citable.
CrossRef is the innovative multi-publisher reference linking system enabling readers to move seamlessly from a reference in a journal article to the cited publication, typically located on a different server and published by a different publisher.

How can I access Wiley InterScience?

Visit http://www.interscience.wiley.com

Guest Users can browse Wiley InterScience for unrestricted access to journal Tables of Contents and Article Abstracts, or use the powerful search engine.
Registered Users are provided with a *Personal Home Page* to store and manage customized alerts, searches, and links to favorite journals and articles. Additionally, Registered Users can view free Online Sample Issues and preview selected material from major reference works.
Licensed Customers are entitled to access full-text journal articles in PDF, with select journals also offering full-text HTML.

How do I become an Authorized User?

Authorized Users are individuals authorized by a paying Customer to have access to the journals in Wiley InterScience. For example, a university that subscribes to Wiley journals is considered to be the Customer. Faculty, staff and students authorized by the university to have access to those journals in Wiley InterScience are Authorized Users. Users should contact their Library for information on which Wiley journals they have access to in Wiley InterScience.

ASK YOUR INSTITUTION ABOUT WILEY INTERSCIENCE TODAY!